Johannes Peter Müller

On certain variations in the vocal organs of the Passeres that have hitherto escaped notice

Johannes Peter
Mu
..
ller

On certain variations in the vocal organs of the Passeres that have hitherto escaped notice

ISBN/EAN: 9783337724498

Printed in Europe, USA, Canada, Australia, Japan

Cover: Foto ©ninafisch / pixelio.de

More available books at **www.hansebooks.com**

JOHANNES MÜLLER
ON CERTAIN VARIATIONS
IN THE
VOCAL ORGANS
OF THE
PASSERES
THAT HAVE HITHERTO ESCAPED NOTICE

THE TRANSLATION
BY
F. JEFFREY BELL, B.A.
EXHIBITIONER OF MAGDALEN COLLEGE, OXFORD

EDITED, WITH AN APPENDIX
BY
A. H. GARROD, M.A., F.R.S.
FELLOW OF ST. JOHN'S COLLEGE, CAMBRIDGE

Oxford
AT THE CLARENDON PRESS
M DCCC LXXVIII

Price Seven Shillings and Sixpence

F W

JOHANNES MÜLLER

ON CERTAIN VARIATIONS IN THE VOCAL ORGANS OF THE PASSERES THAT HAVE HITHERTO ESCAPED NOTICE.

Read before the Königl. Akademie der Wissenschaften zu Berlin.

May 14, 1846, and June 26, 1848.

London

MACMILLAN AND CO.

PUBLISHERS TO THE UNIVERSITY OF

Oxford

JOHANNES MÜLLER

ON CERTAIN VARIATIONS

IN THE

VOCAL ORGANS

OF THE

PASSERES

THAT HAVE HITHERTO ESCAPED NOTICE

THE TRANSLATION

BY

F. JEFFREY BELL, B.A.

EXHIBITIONER OF MAGDALEN COLLEGE, OXFORD

EDITED, WITH AN APPENDIX

BY

A. H. GARROD, M.A., F.R.S.

FELLOW OF ST. JOHN'S COLLEGE, CAMBRIDGE

Oxford

AT THE CLARENDON PRESS

M DCCC LXXVIII

FW

[*All rights reserved*]

PREFACE.

THAT many of the results recorded in this volume are, even after the many years which have elapsed since they were brought before the notice of the scientific world, but little known in this country; that through the kind efforts of Mr. P. L. Sclater, F.R.S., and the willing aid of Dr. W. Peters of Berlin, the originals of Müller's plates were placed at our disposal; and that the Delegates of the Clarendon Press accepted the responsibility of publishing it; are our justifications for the production of the translation of this valuable monograph.

A. H. G.
F. J. B.

July 3rd, 1878.

CONTENTS.

		PAGE
I.	HISTORICAL REMARKS ON THE DISTINCTION BETWEEN SINGING BIRDS AND OTHER PASSERINES, FOUNDED ON THEIR VOCAL MUSCLES	1
II.	REVIEW OF THE GENERA THE LARYNGES OF WHICH HAVE BEEN ALREADY EXAMINED	5
III.	NEW INVESTIGATIONS INTO THE ARRANGEMENT OF THE VOCAL MUSCLES, IN THE OLD AND NEW WORLD FORMS	9
IV.	ACCOUNT OF OBSERVED FORMS OF LARYNX:	
	(i) Organ of Voice of *Chasmarhynchus*	21
	(ii) Organ of Voice of the *Piprinae*	24
	(iii) Organ of Voice of the *Ampelinae* and *Eurylaiminae*	25
	(iv) Organ of Voice of the *Tyranninae* and *Fluvicolinae*	27
	(v) Organ of Voice of the *Todinae* and *Platyrhynchinae*, Cab.	29
	(vi) Organ of Voice of the *Myiotherinae, Scytalopinae, Anabatinae,* and *Dendrocolaptinae*	30
	(vii) Organ of Voice of *Trochilus*	37
	(viii) Organ of Voice of *Colius*	37
V.	ON THE RELATIONS BETWEEN THE STRUCTURE OF THE ORGAN OF VOICE, AND THE EXTERNAL CHARACTERS OF THE PASSERINES	38
VI.	GENERAL REMARKS ON THE CLASSIFICATION OF THE PASSERINES	45
	REMARKS	53
	DESCRIPTION OF THE FIGURES	54
	ADDENDUM TO MÜLLER'S PAPER ON THE VOCAL ORGANS OF PASSERINE BIRDS	61
	APPENDIX CONTAINING A DESCRIPTION OF THE VOCAL ORGANS OF SOME ABERRANT PASSERINE BIRDS NOT RECORDED BY MÜLLER	63

PASSERES.

I. HISTORICAL REMARKS ON THE DISTINCTION BETWEEN SINGING BIRDS AND OTHER PASSERINES, FOUNDED ON THEIR VOCAL MUSCLES.

CUVIER[1] was the first to give a description of the organ of voice, or lower larynx of Singing Birds, and to his work every one has since had recourse. According to him, Singing Birds possess a muscular organ of voice made up of five muscles on each side of the lower larynx, which arise from it and from the trachea, and pass obliquely downwards, partly to the anterior, and partly to the posterior ends of the highly moveable half-rings of the bronchi, raising the second and third half-rings by their anterior and posterior extremeties, and altering their position, as well as that of the vocal cords, with respect to the stream of air.

These muscles are the long anterior and posterior elevators of the third half-ring; the small *constrictor longitudinalis*, which is attached to the posterior elevator, and to the second half-ring; the *constrictor obliquus*, which also moves the hinder extremity of the second half-ring, and the *constrictor transversalis*, which goes to the anterior end of the same half-ring.

This group of muscles is characterised by the fact, that they work not on the middle convex portion of the half-rings, but on their ends, to which they diverge forwards and backwards after leaving the sides of the trachea. The consequence of this division of the moving force is a complete change of position, and a rotation of the half-rings, as described by Savart, which is consequent on the raising of their ends. It is not my aim to describe the mechanism of this larynx or of its cords, *membrana tympaniformis* and *cartilago arytaenoidea*, which latter is so often present in this region, nor the other parts which may be observed here, since they may be supposed to be known from the descriptions of Cuvier and Savart. Cuvier found this complex muscular organ of voice in Sparrows, Titmice, Blackbirds, Thrushes, Buntings, Larks, Ravens, Rooks, Nuthatches,

---

[1] Magasin encyclopaedique ou journal des sciences, des lettres et des arts, redigé par Noel et Warens, T. II. N. VII. p. 330; Reil's Archiv f. Phys. V. p. 67.

B

and Magpies, and asserted that it was generally present in the Passerines with the exception of the Swifts (*Cypselus*), Goatsuckers, and Kingfishers, which, like many birds not placed among Passerines, but belonging to the *Accipitres*, *Scansores*, and *Palmipedes*, possess only a single median muscle on either side of the lower larynx. Tiedemann[1] and Meckel[2] confirmed these results, but pursued the subject no further. Savart[3] confirmed them in essential points, but did pursue the subject; he described six muscles, three anterior and three posterior pairs, in the Ravens, Shrikes, and Starlings, and five (two anterior pairs) in the Thrushes and Larks. In Naumann's work on the Birds of Germany, Nitzsch pointed out the presence of the muscular organ of voice in every genus of European Songster which he had been able to examine. In his different ornithological Essays, for example in those on the nasal glands of birds[4], and on the carotids[5], in his Anatomical Appendices to Naumann's work[6], in his posthumous notes [Article 'Passerinen' by Burmeister, in Ersch and Gruber's Encyclopaedia], and in his Pterylographie[7], he attempts to separate those Passerines which do not possess this complex organ of voice, but possess only one muscle, like the majority of the *Scansores*, from the Singing Birds or Passerines, and to unite them with the *Scansores* into one order of Wood-peckers (Spechtvögel) or *Picariae*. He sought eagerly after other osteological, splanchnological, and angeiological characters of Singing Birds; and in this way many interesting peculiarities in and differences among them were brought to light. But it can be seen at the same time that no one of these characters is absolute, and that there are important exceptions to each of them. Many birds, in which the muscular organ of voice is absent, have the manubrium of the sternum bifurcate, as *Ampelis*, *Gymnocephalus*, *Rupicola*, *Pipra*, *Furnarius*, *Thamnophilus*, *Tyrannus*, *Elaenia*, and many others. No Passerine, it is well known, with two notches on each side of the sternum, possesses the muscular organ of voice; but the sternum of very many Passerines, in which I have not found the muscular organ of voice, has only one notch on each side, e. g. *Eurylaimus*, *Ampelis*, *Gymnocephalus*, *Psaris*, *Pachyrhamphus*, *Phibalura*, *Rupicola*, *Pipra*, *Tyrannus*, *Elaenia*, *Myiobius*, *Fluvicola*, *Thamnophilus*, *Myiothera*, *Tinactor*, *Furnarius*, *Cinclodes*, *Chamaeza*, *Conopophaga*, *Synallaxis*, *Xenops*, *Anabates*, *Dendrocolaptes*, and others.

---

[1] Zoologie. II. Band. Heidelberg, 1810, p. 669.
[2] Syst. d. vergl. Anat. VI. Halle, 1833, p. 488.
[3] Froriep's Notizen. XVI. Band. 1826, N. 331.
[4] Meckels Deutsches Archiv f. d. Physiologie, VI. 234.
[5] Obs. de avium arteria carotide communi. Halae, 1829. 4.
[6] Naturgeschichte der Vögel Deutschlands. Leipz. 1822.
[7] System der Pterylographie. Halle, 1840. 4.

These osteological differences are no more important in the Passerines than in the Gallinaceae. As in the latter there are genera with one notch, as *Crypturus* and *Hemipodius;* and with two; so are there among the Passerines species with one notch, and others with two (*Pteroptochus, Scytalopus, Colius, Coracias, Eurystomus, Merops, Prionites, Alcedo*); and while this notch may become a foramen, as in *Ampelis*, the sternum in some cases becomes quite solid, as in *Trochilus* and *Cypselus*. In this same natural family, as in the family of *Tracheophoni*, discovered by me, there are genera with one notch in the sternum, as *Thamnophilus, Myiothera, Tinactor, Furnarius, Cinclodes, Chamaeza, Conopophaga, Synallaxis, Xenops, Anabates, Dendrocolaptes;* while there are, on the other hand, closely related genera with two, as *Pteroptochus* and *Scytalopus*. It is just the same in the genus *Todus* L.; *Todirostrum* Less., and *Orchilus* Cab. (*Todus megacephalus* Sw.), have only one notch, while the true *Todus* (*T. viridis* L.) has two notches in the sternum.

Nitzsch considered that the genera *Trochilus, Cypselus, Caprimulgus, Coracias, Upupa, Merops,* and *Alcedo* did not conform to the Passerine type; and he separated *Cypselus* from *Hirundo*, which latter possesses the muscular organ of voice, into quite different orders of birds. In his paper on the Carotids he errs slightly, through considering only the genera which should be separated from the Singing Birds, and not those which should be left with them. Among the false Passerines out of *Trochilus, Cypselus,* and *Hemiprocne* he formed his Family *Macrochires;* out of the genera *Upupa, Buceros, Epimachus* (?) and *Alcedo,* his *Lipoglossae;* out of *Caprimulgus, Nyctornis, Podargus, Coracias,* and *Merops,* together with some of the Scansores—*Galbula, Cuculus, Phoenicophaeus, Coccygius, Centropus, Crotophaga, Scythrops, Leptosomatus, Indicator, Trogon*—his family *Cuculinae.* Then follow the *Psittacidae,* and finally the *Amphibolae: Musophaga, Colius,* and *Opisthocomus.*

In the System of Pterylography Nitzsch carried his classification further by the aid of the not very useful 'feather-tracts;' he was obliged to assign a position to all the birds which he took for Singing Birds, but as he based his arrangement of the genera of which he did not know the larynges, on other grounds, he must have erred through the untenableness of his assumptions.

His division of Singing Birds contains a large number of genera which possess no singing muscles; his division of *Picariae* consists of the *Macrochires, Caprimulginae, Todidae, Cuculinae, Picinae, Psittacinae, Lipoglossae,* and *Amphibolae.*

The very useful anatomical work of Nitzsch gave, as was natural, great weight to his systematic views, and consequently they have been recognised, and accepted, by eminent zoologists in Germany. A. Wagner, Burmeister, Count Keyserling, and Blasius have followed them; and although Wagler in his Classification of Birds has made but little use of Nitzsch's work, he has called Nitzsch the Master of Ornithologists, so far has his authority extended.

Later on, Blyth [1] put forward views similar to those of Nitzsch, as to the necessity of separating the Singing Birds from the false Passerines. As the internal differences between Singing Birds and the *Picariae* were regarded as thoroughly established, several ornithologists directed their energies to discovering the external differences between these divisions. Keyserling and Blasius [2] fancied that they could recognise a striking difference in the covering of the feet of the Singing Birds and *Picariae;* and indeed, within certain limits, this peculiarity does enable us to form conclusions as to internal structure. The exceptions, which Burmeister [3] pointed out, may for the greater part be disregarded, as the genera which appear to form the exceptions were, for the most part, wrongly classified by Nitzsch. But the birds whose larynges I have examined offer some very striking and inexplicable exceptions to the law discovered by Keyserling and Blasius, and in these cases as to the structure of the larynx, a wrong conclusion would be arrived at from the characters of the foot. I shall return to this subject in the systematic portion of this treatise.

Sundevall has lately discovered a difference in the arrangement of the wing feathers, and has made use of it in the separation of Singing Birds and *Picariae* (*Coccyges* Sund.); this difference may have its value, as a characteristic of families and genera, but can possess no greater. The separation of Singing Birds and *Picariae*, according to an internal difference described by Nitzsch, is untenable for a large number of genera, after my researches into the organ of voice and other parts. The vocal organ in the Passerine birds is by no means so exactly constructed upon two principal types, for there are no doubt a greater number of peculiar forms, the most important variations of which are as yet unknown; and it will be only after a complete knowledge of these that the question of the classification of the Passerines can be again taken up with success. Later classifications of birds are no better than those of Nitzsch. Vieillot, Cuvier, Temminck, Vigors, Swainson, Wagler, Boie, and Gray have done excellent work in increasing our knowledge of the genera of birds, but their classifications are not based upon scientific principles; they bring birds together into a family according only to their own opinions, so that we can scarcely wonder at their families being of no more value than irrational groups without characters, nor that those groups vary with different authors. The works

---

[1] Mag. Nat. Hist. Vol. II.
[2] Wiegmann's Archiv, 1839, I. 332. K. and B. die Wirbelthiere Europa's, 1840.
[3] Wiegmann's Archiv, 1840, I. 220. Cf. K. and B. ibid. p. 362.

of Nitzsch and his followers start at least from earnest inquiries into the structure of birds; he was for a long time the only man who struggled for the goal, but he did not find it.

II. REVIEW OF THE GENERA THE LARYNGES OF WHICH HAVE BEEN ALREADY EXAMINED.

The investigations of Cuvier were altogether limited to the European Passerines; of those without the muscular organ of voice he only examined *Alcedo, Caprimulgus, Cypselus, Coracias,* and *Upupa*. Nitzsch observed the complex muscular organ of voice in the European genera *Lanius, Turdus, Sturnus, Muscicapa, Corvus, Bombycilla, Oriolus, Fringilla, Pyrrhula, Emberiza, Saxicola, Accentor, Regulus, Troglodytes, Anthus, Motacilla, Parus, Cinclus, Hirundo, Alauda, Certhia,* and *Sitta*. His investigations on European Passerines without the complex organ of voice were made on *Alcedo, Caprimulgus, Cypselus, Coracias, Upupa,* and *Merops*. In his investigations on the carotids he only made use of the non-European genera *Nectarinia, Crateropus* (*Sphenura acaciae* Licht.), *Caereba,* and *Icterus,* which possess vocal muscles, and *Trochilus,* which is without them.

What Nitzsch did for European birds, Audubon did for those of North America in the fifth volume of his 'Ornithological Biography,' Edin. 1839. Fully impressed with the importance of this investigation, and convinced of the uselessness of the work of those who founded their classification on the skins of birds ('Dry-skin Philosophers¹'), he examined the larynx and digestive organs of a large number of North American birds, among which were many Passerines. He found the muscular organ of voice, with four muscles, in the genera *Lanius, Vireo, Turdus, Sturnus, Icterus, Fringilla, Tanagra, Parus, Sylvia, Hirundo,* and *Alauda*. The Thrushes examined by him belong to the genera *Seiurus, Mimus,* and *Icteria;* the Starlings to *Quiscalus, Sturnella, Scolecophagus;* the Icteridae to the genera *Icterus, Yphantes, Agelaius, Molothrus;* the Fringillidae to the genera *Chrysomitris, Corythus, Spizella, Ammodramus, Passerella, Spiza, Erythrospiza, Loxia, Coturniculus;* the Sylvidae to the genera *Myiodioctes, Sialia, Trichas, Sylvicola, Vermivora, Regulus, Thryothorus, Troglodytes,* and *Anthus*. Of the Passerines without the muscular organ of voice the American *Muscicapidae* were first made known by him. The genera forming his Muscicapidae are *Tyrannus* Sw. (*M. tyrannus*), *Tyrannula* Sw. (*M. crinita*), and *Setophaga* Sw. (*M. ruticilla*).

---

[1] Loc. cit. V. 547.

The numerical relation of the so-called false Passerines to the Singing Birds appears from his investigations to be pretty much the same in North America as in Europe and the Old World. *Alcedo, Cypselus,* and *Caprimulgus*[1] belong to both worlds; instead of *Upupa, Merops, Coracias,* and *Eurystomus,* there appear in the New World *Trochilus, Tyrannus, Tyrannula,* and *Setophaga;* the great majority of Passerines, both in the Old World and in North America, belong to the true Singing Birds.

Prince Max von Neuwied, Eyton, v. Tschudi, and myself have described several of the South American Passerines with reference to their organs of voice.

Prince Max gave a figure[2] of the external appearance of the lower larynx of *Chasmorhynchus nudicollis,* from which it can be seen that the organ of this bird is very muscular, but it leaves it doubtful whether the organ belongs to the so-called muscular organ of voice.

Blyth finds the muscular organ of voice in the *Cotingidae* and Manakins[3]; he says that he has opened several broad-billed *Tyrannidae* and that they all possess the characters of Singing Birds[4]; and that *Phytotoma* is in all structural peculiarities a Singing Bird[5]. But it is certain that neither the *Cotingidae,* Manakins, or *Tyrannidae* possess the muscular organ of voice; all the genera of these birds which I have examined wanting it.

Eyton makes in the Appendix to Darwin's Zoology of the Voyage of H.M.S. Beagle, part iii, Birds, London 1841–4, some anatomical remarks on *Serpophaga albocoronata, Furnarius cunicularius, Upucerthia dumetoria, Opetiorhynchus vulgaris, O. antarcticus, O. patagonicus, Pteroptochos Tarnii, P. albicollis, Synallaxis maluroides, Phytotoma rara,* and *Trochilus gigas.*

A. Wagner expresses in his Jahresbericht[6] his regret that Eyton had only directed his attention to the Sterno-tracheal muscles, and not to the proper muscles of the lower larynx also; and really, his information on the organ of voice of genera, then examined for the first time, is very meagre and unsatisfactory. It is said of *Serpophaga* that the trachea is supplied with the same muscles as in Songsters. Of *Phytotoma* he says, Trachea with one pair of Sterno-tracheal muscles; and further on we learn nothing more than that the skeleton as well as the soft parts resemble those of the genus *Loxia.* Eydoux and Souleyet[7] have quite overlooked the larynx in their

---

[1] The North-American forms of *Cypselus (Acanthylis* Boie), *Caprimulgus (Antrostomus* Gould), and *Chordeiles* (Sw.) were examined by Audubon.
[2] Beiträge zur Naturgeschichte von Brasilien, B. III. fig. 1.
[3] Mag. Nat. Hist. Vol. II. p. 264.   [4] Ibid. p. 360.   [5] Ibid. p. 600.
[6] Erichson's Archiv, 1841, II. p. 64.
[7] Voyage autour du monde sur la corvette la Bonite. Paris. Zoologie, T. I. p. 92.

anatomical notes on *Phytotoma*. Since *Phytotoma* belongs to the *Ampelidae*, according to the structure of the foot, it may be said beforehand with great probability, that the larynx does not resemble that of *Loxia*. *Phytotoma* is in all probability not a Singing Bird. Of *Upucerthia dumetoria* Eyton says: the trachea with one pair of sterno-tracheal muscles. From the upper ring of each bronchus, a process goes to the place where the muscles arise. Only as far as this do the rings of the trachea reach, and beyond it are two spaces, devoid of osseous matter, and bounded laterally by the processes above-mentioned, inferiorly by the upper rings of the bronchi, and superiorly by the lower ring of the trachea, which is slightly enlarged. As well as the fine vibrating anterior and posterior half-rings, in this portion of the trachea there are the elastic bands, which fasten these half-rings, and pass under the two true laryngeal muscles of either side; moreover, it is incorrect to say that the membranous portion of the trachea is connected with the processes of the bronchi. In *Furnarius cunicularius* the trachea is as in *Opetiorhynchus (Cinclodes) vulgaris*, and *O. (Cinclodes) antarcticus*. In *O. (Cinclodes) patagonicus*, the trachea does not differ from the usual simple form found in most other birds, the inferior rings reaching as far as the bronchi, which arrangement is different from that found in *O. vulgaris* and *O. antarcticus*; the trachea has one pair of muscles. In *Synallaxis maluroides* the trachea is the same as in *Furnarius* and *Upucerthia*. In *Pteroptochus tarnii* the trachea is provided with a pair of sterno-tracheal muscles, a portion of which is prolonged to the upper bronchial rings.

Since *Scytalopus*, which is closely allied to *Pteroptochus*, has no tracheal larynx, according to my observations, it may be fairly presumed that the information about *Pteroptochus* also is not sufficient. Eyton has given us more exact information about some birds from New Holland.

The vocal organ of the Guacharo, *Steatornis caripensis*, has been described and figured by myself[1]. It is without the complex vocal muscles, and possesses a peculiarity, of which till now no example has been known among birds. At the lower end of the trachea there is no lower larynx, the bronchi have the same structure as the trachea, that is perfect rings, the left bronchus has sixteen, the right eleven, perfect rings reaching as far as the organ of voice, which is a bronchial larynx, and is thus double. The ring that follows on these bronchial rings is thicker, and not perfect, after which there is a thicker half-ring with the under edge concave, on which the vocal muscle works. The outer wall between it and the next half-ring, which has its upper edge convex, is

---

[1] Bericht der Akad. d. Wissenschaft z. Berlin 1841, p. 172; Müll. Archiv, 1842, p. 1.

membranous, and forms the outer membrane of the tympanum, between the concavities of these two rings; further on are half-rings. The simple vocal muscle arises from the end of the trachea, where the lateral muscle of the trachea stops. The sternotracheal muscles are of the usual form.

In the same paper is a notice of the larynx of *Opisthocomus cristatus*, which has no muscles[1].

V. Tschudi has described the trachea and organ of voice of *Cephalopterus ornatus*[2]. He points out that the trachea widens into a flattened tympanum 14''' long, and 7''' broad, shortly beyond the upper larynx. Before the widening it has a diameter of 3''', after it of 2'''. The vocal muscle is simple, arises from the end of the trachea, and is inserted into the fourth half-ring of the bronchi.

Of the forms of Passerines peculiar to Africa, I have described the organ of voice in *Colius* and *Corythaix*[3]. *Colius* has a simple thick vocal muscle: *Corythaix* has no laryngeal muscle.

Of the forms peculiar to the East Indies, and the Sunda Islands, we still know very little. Stannius[4] has described the larynx of *Podargus*; it has one simple muscle, as in the allied *Caprimulgus*.

Of the Australian Singing Birds Eyton has only examined a few species, namely *Menura lyra*, *Cracticus tibicen*, and *Psophodes crepitans*[5]. *Menura* is peculiar. Besides the usual sternotracheal muscles it has two pairs of laryngeal muscles, the anterior inserted into the end of the fourth bronchial ring; the posterior into the three upper rings, and the posterior ends of the fifth. The muscles are very strong. The author remarks, that *Menura* agrees in the structure of its soft parts with the *Insessores*, and especially with *Grallina* in the complex muscular arrangement of the lower larynx; but the larynx of *Grallina* is not known, and it would have been well if the author had described its muscles. *Psophodes crepitans* V. H. has five pairs of muscles, as have the Rooks and Warblers; *Cracticus tibicen* resembles the *Corvidae* in its vocal muscles. The supposition that the anatomy of the South American genus *Thamnophilus*, which Eyton has not examined, agrees with *Psophodes*, is not correct.

Lesson and Garnot have examined two of the rare birds of New Guinea, *Phonygama*

---

[1] Bericht der Akad. d. Wissenschaft z. Berlin, 1841, p. 177; Müll. Archiv, 1842, p. 10.
[2] Archiv f. Anat. u. Physiol. 1843, p. 473.
[3] Bericht der Akad. d. Wissenschaft z. Berlin, 1841, p. 179; Müll. Archiv, 1842, p. 11.
[4] Lehrb. d. Vergl. Anat. II. 2, Berlin, 1846, p. 321.
[5] Annals of Nat. Hist. Vol. III, 1841, p. 49, VIII. p. 46.

keraudrenii Less[1] and *Paradisea apoda*[2]. Of the former they have only mentioned the windings of the trachea beneath the skin of the abdomen, and thorax, but have forgotten the larynx, and their description of the trachea with its muscles is unintelligible.

III. New Investigations into the Arrangement of the Vocal Muscles, in the Old and New World Forms.

Having been for a very long time convinced that there still remained much to be done in the classification of birds by the aid of Anatomy, and that Cuvier had left this portion of his Règne Animal quite unfinished, I have for many years striven to collect a large number of birds, in spirit, for this purpose. I have lately also studied the Passerines in the Anatomical Museum. The first object that I placed before myself, was to learn the arrangement of the vocal muscles. And thus, at the same time, new facts presented themselves, which led further than this aim of mine. As regards the Passerines of the Old World the views put forward by Nitzsch have not been changed in any essential particulars : I have met, among them, with no other forms of larynx than the muscular organ of voice, and the larynx of the so-called *Picariae* with only one muscle. I have examined seventy-two genera of the Singing Birds of the Old World with the muscular organ of voice. The number of Passerines of the Old World without the muscular organ of voice is, on the contrary, very small; namely, *Cypselus*, *Caprimulgus*, *Podargus*, *Coracias*, *Eurystomus*, *Eurylaimus*, *Colius*, *Alcedo*, *Merops*, *Upupa*, and *Buceros*, to which probably *Calyptomena* should be also added, although this genus has not yet been examined. As regards the New World, and especially South America, my views about the Singing Birds and *Picariae* have been completely changed. I have examined over one hundred genera of Passerines from America. The larynx, without the muscular organ of voice, of the kind peculiar to the *Picariae*, is found among very many of the American genera of Singing Birds. Almost the half of all the genera of American Passerines examined—without counting the *Scansores*—are not Singing Birds with the muscular organ of voice, according to my observations. The majority of them have only the simple Picarian larynx ; but there are among them peculiar and more complex larynges with one, or more than one muscle, which are very different from the so-called muscular organ of voice, and formed on quite another principle. Finally the most complex musculature, so far as the number of muscles is concerned, is that

---

[1] Voyage autour du monde sur la corvette la Coquille par Duperrey. Zoologie. Paris, 1826,.p. 636.
[2] Ib. p. 596.

found in the so-called muscular organ of voice; but there is a far more muscular form of voice-organ which produces tones in the highest degree harmonious and capable of modulation, and yet is totally unlike in structure the so-called muscular organ of voice.

Most of the so-called Ampelidae of the Picarian type (Nitzsch) have only one muscle, and are not Singing Birds. *Gymnocephalus* (*G. calvus*), *Ampelis* or *Cotinga* (*A. pompadora*), *Rupicola* (*R. cayana*), and *Phibalura* resemble *Cephalopterus*. All these birds have only one, very slender, laryngeal muscle, which looks like a prolongation of the lateral muscle of the trachea.

The hitherto complex and varied family of the *Ampelidae* contains moreover birds with the muscular organ of voice—viz. *Bombycilla;* and further contains the most extreme form of larynx known in birds, although constructed on a different model; viz. *Chasmarhynchus*.

The genus *Lanius* Cuv., which belongs to the family, contains Singing Birds, and *Picariae*, mixed up with one another. The European, African, and American *Lani*, and the Australian *Barita*, or more correctly *Gymnorhina* Gray (*G. tibicen*), are birds with vocal muscles. The genera *Psaris*, *Pachyrhamphus*, and *Thamnophilus* have no muscular organ of voice. Of the true Shrikes with vocal muscles, America possesses only *Lanius*, *Vireo*, and *Cyclorhis* Sw., of which the first two come from North America. *Cyclorhis* is the sole representative of this family in South America. *Thamnophilus* Vieill., of which Cuvier knew so little, that he placed it with the true *Lanii*, has only one laryngeal muscle, but a perfectly peculiar larynx in the trachea itself, which brings it closer to several American Passerines, which have been placed with the Fly-catchers, Thrushes, Wrens, and Tree-creepers. The sub-family *Thamnophilini* should not be placed with these, since *Malaconotus* Sw. completely agrees, in its muscular organ of voice, with the true *Lanii*. This genus *Malaconotus* is exceedingly ill defined, as are so many that have been made without a knowledge of their anatomy. Indeed the single muscle, and the peculiar larynx of *Thamnophilus* are found again in *Myiothera*, *Conopophaga*, and *Chamaeza*, which have been placed with the Thrushes, or the Ant-catchers, of the Old World.

Furnarius, *Cinclodes*, *Synallaxis*, *Xenops*, *Anabates*, *Tinactor*, and *Dendrocolaptes*, which have been partly placed with the Thrushes and partly with the Tree-creepers, have two laryngeal muscles on either side, while the peculiar larynx situated in their trachea, unites them closely to *Thamnophilus*, *Myiothera*, *Conopophaga*, *Chamaeza*, and *Scytalopus*.

The genus *Muscicapa* Cuv. presents great differences from the arrangement found in *Lanius* Cuv., and *Certhia* Cuv. The *Muscicapidae* of the Old World, *Muscicapa* in the narrowest sense, both the European, Asiatic, and African forms, as well as the African *Muscipeta* Sw., and *Platystera* Jard. Selb. possess the complex muscular organ of voice of Singing Birds. The American *Muscicapidae*, or *Tyrannidae*, have no muscular organ of voice, but only one muscle, which may be thick, as in *Tyrannus, Saurophagus, Tyrannula*, and *Elaenia*, or very thin as in *Myiobius, Arundinicola, Pyrocephalus, Todirostrum*, and others.

The genus *Culicivora* Sw. (*Sylvia bivittata* Mus. Berol.), which is provided with a muscular organ of voice, would make an exception, and would be the sole representative of the *Muscicapa* of the Old World, in North America, and America generally, if this genus belongs to the *Muscicapinae*, with which Gray places it. But *Culicivora* appears to have been more correctly placed by Swainson with the *Sylvianae* in consequence of the presence of this organ.

The *Fluvicolinae* have only a single vocal muscle. The *Piprinae* also have not the complex muscular organ of voice, but a single vocal muscle, sometimes thicker, sometimes thinner.

The following is a list of all the genera of American Passerines without the complex muscular organ of voice, which I have examined.

Chasmarhynchus Temm.
Cotinga Briss.
Gymnocephalus Geoffr.
Rupicola Briss.
Phibalura Vieill.
Pipra L.
Jodopleura Less.
Calyptura Sw.
Psaris Cuv.
Pachyrhamphus Gray.
Tyrannus Cuv.
Saurophagus Sw.
Machetornis Gray.
Tyrannula Sw.
Platyrhynchus Desm.
Elaenia Sund.
Myiobius Gray.
Arundinicola Cab.

Pyrocephalus Gould.
Fluvicola Sw.
Centrites Cab. (*Alauda rufa* aut.)
Colopterus Cab., n.g.
Orchilus Cab. (*Todus megacephalus* Sw.)
Todirostrum Less.
Todus L.
Thamnophilus Vieill.
Myiothera Ill.
Conopophaga Vieill.
Chamaeza Vig.
Tinactor Pr. Max.
Furnarius Vieill.
Cinclodes Gray.
Synallaxis Vieill.
Xenops Hoffm.
Anabates Temm.
Dendrocolaptes Herm.

Scytalopus Gould.	*Cypselus* Ill.
Phaëtornis Sw.	*Caprimulgus* L.
Orthorhynchus Cuv.	*Steatornis* Humb.
Ornismyia Less.	*Alcedo* L.
Lampornis Sw.	*Prionites* Ill.
Campylopterus Sw.	*Opisthocomus* Hoffm.

If the genera *Setophaga* Sw., *Cephalopterus* Geoffr., and *Pteroptochus* Kittl., be classed with the above, there are as many as fifty genera of the Passerine order already known as wanting the muscular vocal larynx, of which the greater number are South American. I am acquainted with sixty-four American genera, which conform to the type of the European Singing Birds; namely, *Lanius*, *Fringilla*, *Tanagra*, *Sylvia*, *Hirundo*, *Cassicus*, *Turdus*, *Quiscalus*, *Sturnella*, *Caereba*, *Dacnis*, *Troglodytes*, and their subgenera. If we reckon the American *Scansores* as *Picariae*, in Nitzsch's sense, in addition to the already mentioned fifty genera, the number of *Picariae* in the New World will amount to more than half of all the Insessores of this hemisphere, that have been observed. And this explains the well-known fact that the forests of tropical America resound much more with cries than songs.

In the Old World, that is in Europe, Asia, and Africa, there are to my knowledge seventy-two genera of Passerines with a vocal larynx, but there are only nine *Picariae*—without reckoning *Scansores*—namely:

Upupa L.	*Cypselus* Ill.
Alcedo L.	*Caprimulgus* L.
Coracias L.	*Podargus* Cuv.
Eurystomus Vieill.	*Colius* Briss.
Eurylaimus Horsf.	

There have been only five genera altogether of Passerines from Australia and Polynesia, that have been examined. *Psophodes* and *Gymnorhina*, examined by Eyton, and the latter dissected by myself also, together with the species of *Drepanis* from the Sandwich Islands, which I have examined, appear to be true Singing Birds, while Eyton thinks that *Maenura* and *Grallina* also belong to the group. From my examination of the East Indian genus *Phyllornis*, I have no doubt that the Australian *Meliphagidae* are also true Singing Birds.

The number of birds dissected by me, for my first communication (1845) amounted to some hundreds of species of Passerines, which belonged to about one hundred genera or subgenera. The American forms were obtained in their travels by V. Olfers, Sello,

Deppe, Richard Schomburgk, and v. Winterfeld, the African by Krebs and Peters; many were obtained by purchase, and have been for a long time collected for this purpose; for perfect and undissected animals, preserved in spirit, are of much more value for the progress of science than anatomical preparations of separate parts.

I was enabled from this material to investigate the typical differences in the structure of the larynx of the Passerines, and to settle the matter, of which I gave a full account in the Monatsbericht of the Academy in June, 1845; but it was not sufficient for me to be able to draw from them all those conclusions on the subject of the Classification of Birds, which could be gained from these anatomical facts.

Since that time the number of birds which I have examined has greatly increased. Of several collections, the materials with which my friend Professor Eschricht most kindly supplied me were exceedingly useful in increasing my knowledge as to the distribution of the observed forms of the larynx in America, and in aiding me to draw conclusions as to their classification. I gave an account of my work to the Academy, in an Appendix to my earlier paper. (See the Monatsbericht of the Academy for May, 1846.) I have lately received a great addition to my material from the collection of Indian Birds in spirit, made by Dr. Philippi in Tenasserim. I must also thank Herren Stannius of Rostock and Focke of Bremen for their assistance. It was necessary for the object of the work that the systematic position of the animals to be dissected, not only as regards their species, but also subgenera and synonymy, should be perfectly certain. The author has not dared to rely on his own ornithological knowledge and studies, but an experienced ornithologist of the department, Herr Cabanis, Assistant in the Zoological Museum, from whom we may expect the description of the new birds obtained by Richard Schomburgk in his travels, has compared the spirit specimens with the dried birds in the Zoological Collection, and has named them.

Table of the Genera and Species examined, possessing a Muscular Organ of Voice.
(The Species examined by the Author are marked with an asterisk.)

GENUS.	SUBGENUS.	SPECIES.
Lanius L.	Enneoctonus Boie	L. collurio L.* Cfr. Nitzsch in Naumann, II. 3.
	Lanius L.	L. ludovicianus L. Audub. V. 435.
		L. septentrionalis Gm. Audub. V. 434.
	Laniarius Vieill.	L. cubla Lath.* (Genus Dryoscopus Boie.)
		L. barbarus L.* (Genus Malaconotus Sw.)
		L. bulbul Sh.* (Genus Malaconotus Sw.)
	Telophonus Sw.	L. bakbakiri Sh.*
		L. collaris L.*
	Vireo Vieill.	V. flavifrons V. Audub. V. 428.

Genus.	Subgenus.	Species.
Lanius L.	*Vireo* Vieill.	*V. gilous* Bonap. Ebend. V. 431.
	Cyclorhis Sw.	*C. guianensis* Sw.*
Barita Cuv.	*Gymnorhina* Gray	*Barita tibicen* Cuv.* (Eyton. Mag. Nat. Hist. VIII. 47.)
Pardalotus Vieill.	*Prionochilus* Strickl.	*P.* sp.? *Tenessarim.*
Dicrurus Vieill.	*Dicrurus* V.	*D. musicus* V.* (*Muscicapa emarginata* Licht. Doubl. Verz. 544.)
		Edolius griseus Temm.*
		E. longus Temm.*
Campephaga V.	*Campephaga* V.	*Muscicapa labrosa*, Sw.*
Turdus L.	*Merula* Boie	*T. merula* Nitzsch.
	Turdus L.	*T. viscivorus, musicus, pilaris, torquatus*, Nitzsch.
		T. carbonarius, Licht.* (*flavipes* Spix.)
		T. rufiventris Spix.*
		T. migratorius L. Audub. V. 442.
		T. minor Gm. Ebend. 445.
		T. mustelinus Gm. Ebend. 446.
		T. Wilsonii Bonap. Ebend. 446.
	Petrocossyphus Boie	*T. cyanus* L.*
		T. manilensis L. Gm.*
	Seiurus Sw.	*T. aquaticus* Wils. in Audub. V. 284.
		T. auricapillus Lath. Ebend. 447.
	Crateropus Sw.	*Sphenura acaciae* Licht.* Doubl. Verz. 454.
	Mimus Boie	*T. polyglottus* L. Audub. V. 438.
		T. felivox Vieill. Ebend. V. 440.
		T. rufus L. Ebend. 441.
		T. rubripes Temm.*
	Ixos Temm.	*T. capensis* L.*
		T. atriceps Temm.*
		T. xanthopygus Mus. Berol.*
		Lanius jocosus L. Gm.*
Sturnus L.	*Sturnus* L.	*S. vulgaris* L. Nitzsch in Naumann II. 186.
	Quiscalus Vieill.	*Q.* spec. Guian.*
		Q. versicolor V. in Audub. V. 481.
		Q. major V. Ebend. 480.
	Sturnella Vieill.	*Sturnus ludovicianus* L. in Audub. V. 492.
	Scolecophagus Sw.	*Quiscalus ferrugineus* Bonap. Audub. V. 483.
	Dilophus Vieill.	*Gracula carunculata* Gm.*
		Sturnus capensis L.*
		Pastor caniceps Hodgs.*
		Gracula sturnina Gm.*
	Eulabes Cuv.	*E. religiosa* C.*
	Lamprotornis T.	*Turdus morio* L.*
		T. auratus L. Gm.*
Muscicapa L.	*Muscicapa* Sw.	*M. atricupilla* L.*
		M. grisola L.* Cf. Nitzsch in Naumann. II. 216.
		M. atroniteus Mus. Berol.* Mozamb.

Genus.	Subgenus.	Species.
Muscicapa L.	Muscicapa Sw.	M. pondiceriana L. Gm.*
	Muscipeta Sw.	M. paradisi L.*
	Platystera Jard. Selb.	M. succincta Mus. Berol.*
Corvus L.	Corvus Cuv.	C. corax L.* Cf. Nitzsch in Naumann. II. 41.
		C. americanus L. Audub. V. 477.
	Pica Cuv.	C. pica L.*
	Garrulus Cuv.	G. Glandarius C.*
	Cyanocorax Boie	Corvus cristatus L. Audub. V. 475.
	Perisoreus Bonap.	C. canadensis L. Audub. V. 210.
Bombycilla Briss.	Bombycilla Br.	B. garrula Br.* Nitzsch in Naumann. II. 141.
		B. carolinensis Br. Audub. V. 494.
Oriolus L.	Oriolus L.	O. galbula L.* Nitzsch in Naumann. II. 170.
		O. larvatus Licht.* Doubl. Verz. 192.
Cassicus Cuv.	Cassicus C.	C. persicus C.*
	. . . . . .	C. cristatus C.*
	Yphantes Vieill.	Icterus Baltimore Audub. V. 278.
	Icterus C.	I. vulgaris Daud.*
		I. spurius Bonap. Audub. 485.
		I. xanthornus Daud.*
	Xanthornus C.	X. cayennensis C.*
	Chrysomus Sw.	C. icterocephalus Sw.*
	Agelaius Vieill.	Icterus phoeniceus Daud. in. Audub. V. 487.
	Molothrus Sw.	I. pecoris Bonap. in Audub. V. 233.
	Dolichonyx Sw.	D. oryzivorus Sw.*
Fringilla L.	Carduelis Briss.	F. carduelis L. Nitzsch IV. 432.
	Estrelda Sw.	F. bengalus L. Gm.*
	Cannabina Brehm	F. cannabina L. Nitzsch IV. 432.
	Amadina Sw.	Loxia atricapilla Vieill.*
		Amadina spec. Mozamb.*
		F. leuconota Temm.*
	Chrysomitris Boie	F. spinus L. Nitzsch IV. 432.
		F. pinus Wils. in Audub. V. 509.
	Textor T.	Textor malimbus T.*
	Linaria Bechst.	F. linaria L. Nitzsch IV. 432.
	Fringilla Sw.	F. coelebs L. Nitzsch.
		F. montifringilla Ebend.
	Pyrgita Sw.	F. humilis Mus. Berol.*
		F. domestica L. Nitzsch IV. 432.
	Crithagra Sw.	Crithagra spec. Mozamb.*
	Niphaea Aud.	F. hiemalis L. Audub. V. 505.
	Zonotrichia Sw.	F. matutina Licht.* Doubl. Verz.
		F. leucophrys Bonap.*
	Corythus C.	Pyrrhula enucleator Temm. Audub. IV. 414.
	Pyrrhula Cuv.	P. vulgaris T.* Cf. Nitzsch IV. 381.
	Spizella Bonap.	F. canadensis Lath. Audub. V. 404.
	Ploceus C.	P. spinolitus Vig.*

Genus.	Subgenus.	Species.
Fringilla L.	Ploceus C.	P. aurifrons Temm.*
	Ligurinus Briss.	F. chloris L. Nitzsch IV. 432.
	Pithylus Cuv.	F. grossa Gm.*
	Ammodramus Sw.	F. Macgillivrayi Audub. V. 499.
	Coccothraustes Briss.	F. coccothraustes L.* Cf. Nitzsch IV. 432.
	Passerella Sw.	F. iliaca Merr. Audub. V. 512.
	Spiza Bonap.	F. ciris B.*
		F. cyanea Wils. Audub. V. 503.
	Euplectes Sw.	E. spec. Mozamb.*
	Vidua Cuv.	Emberiza paradisea L.*
	Emberiza L.	E. miliaria L. Nitzsch IV. 211.
		E. cirlus L.*
		E. citrinella, hortulana, cia, schoeniclus in Nitzsch IV. 211.
	Plectrophanes Mey.	E. nivalis L.* Cf. Nitzsch IV. 211.
	Erythrospiza Bonap.	F. purpurea Gm. Audub. V. 500.
	Loxia L.	L. curvirostra L.*
		L. pytiopsittacus Bechst. in Nitzsch IV. 338.
		L. leucoptera Gm. Audub. IV. 467.
	Coturniculus Bonap.	F. passerina Wils. in Audub. V. 497.
		F. Brissonii Licht.*
Tanagra L.	Tanagra L.	T. episcopus L.*
		T. sayaca Licht.*
	Icteria Vieill.	I. viridis Bonap. in Audub. V. 433.
	Calospiza Gr.	T. tricolor L. Gm.*
		T. thoracica Temm.*
		T. brasiliensis L.*
	Saltator Vieill.	T. superciliaris Spix.* (Saltator coerulescens Vieill.)
	Rhamphopsis Vieill.	T. jacapa L.*
	Arremon Vieill.	T. silens Lath.*
	Tachyphonus Vieill.	T. loricata Licht.* Doubl. Verz. 340.
		Tachyphonus Vigorsii Sw.* (Tan. coryphaea Licht.)
	Pyranga Vieill.	Tanagra aestiva Gm. in Audub. V. 518.
		T. rubra Elend. IV. 393.
	Tanagrella Sw.	T. archiepiscopus Desm.*
	Procnopis Cab.	T. vittata Temm.*
	Euphone Desm.	T. violacea Licht.*
		T. viridis V.*
	Pipilo Vieill.	Fringilla erythropthalma L. Audub. V. 511.
	Bethylus Cuv.	B. leverianus Cuv.*
Motacilla L.	Zosterops Vig.	Sylvia madagascariensis Lath.*
	Myiodioctes Aud.	S. mitrata Lath. Audub. V. 465.
	Phyllopneuste Mey.	Motacilla trochilus L.*
		M. rufa L.*
	Sialia Sw.	Sylvia sialis Lath. Audub. V. 452.
	Trichas Sw.	S. trichas Lath.* Audub. V. 463.
	Sylvicola Sw.	S. aestiva Lath. Audub. V. 453.

Genus.	Subgenus.	Species.
Motacilla L.	Sylvicola Sw.	S. brasiliana Licht.*
	Culicivora Sw.	S. bivittata Mus. Berol.*
	Dandalus Boie	Motacilla rubecula aut.*
	Hippolais Brehm	M. hippolais L.*
	Saxicola Bechst.	Saxicola oenanthe Bechst.*
		S. superciliaris Mus. Berol. Cap.*
		S. incomta Mus. Berol. Cap.*
		S. rubicola Bechst.* Cf. Nitzsch III. 862.
	Vermivora Sw.	S. ruficapilla Wils.*
		S. vermivora Lath. Audub. V. 460.
	Curruca Bechst.	Motacilla luscinia L.*
	Prinia Horsf.	Prunia sp. Javana.*
	Orthotomus Horsf.	O. sepium?*
	Regulus Ray	R. flavicapillus et ignicapillus Nitzsch III. 967.
		R. tricolor Nutt. Audub. V. 465.
	Jora Horsf.	Sylvia ceylanica Lath.*
	Accentor Bechst.	A. modularis Bechst.* Cf. Nitzsch III. 939.
	Thriothorus Vieill.	Troglodytes ludovicianus Bonap. Audub. V. 466.
	Troglodytes Koch	T. musculus Mus. Berol.* Brazil.
		T. parvulus Koch in Nitzsch III. 724.
		T. hiemalis Vieill. in Audub. IV. 430.
	Campylorhynchus Sp.	C. nuchalis Cab. n. sp.*
	Anthus Bechst.	A. pratensis Bechst.* Cf. Nitzsch III. 744.
		A. pipiens Audub. V. 449.
		A. sp. Tenessarim.*
	Motacilla Bechst.	M. sulphurea Bechst.* Cf. Nitzsch III. 802.
Parus L.	Parus L.	P. luctuosus Licht.* Cf. Nitzsch IV. 7.
		P. bicolor L. Audub. 472.
		P. atricapillus Audub. IV. 374.
	Calamophilus Leach	P. biarmicus Leach *
Timalia Horsf.	Timalia Horsf.	Timalia sp. Tenessarim.*
Cinclus Bechst.	Cinclus Bechst.	C. aquaticus B.* Cf. Nitzsch III. 923.
Hirundo Cuv.	Chelidon Boie	H. urbica L.* Cf. Nitzsch VI. 48.
		H. bicolor Vieill. Audub. V. 417.
	Progne Boie	H. purpurea L.* Audub. V. 411.
	Cotile Boie	H. riparia.
Alauda L.	Alauda L.	A. arvensis L.* Cf. Nitzsch IV. 126.
	Macronyx Sw.	M. flavigaster Sw.*
	Otocoris Bonap.	Alauda alpestris L. Audub. V. 448.
Certhia L.	Certhia L.	C. familiaris L.* Nitzsch V. 396.
Sitta L.	Sitta L.	S. europaea L.* Nitzsch V. 375.
		S. carolinensis Briss. Audub. V. 473.
Nectarinia Ill.	Nectarinia Ill.	Cinnyris senegalensis Cuv.*
		Certhia lepida Sparrm.*
		Cinnyris amethystina Cuv.*
	Arachnothera Temm.	Arachnothera sp. Tenessarim.

Genus.	Subgenus.	Species.
Nectarinia Ill.	Drepanis Temm.	Certhia vestiaria Lath.*
		C. virens Lath.*
		C. sanguinea Lath.*
	Dicaeum Cuv.	Dicaeum sp. Tenesarim.*
Caereba Vieill.	Certhiola Sund.	C. flaveola Sund.*
	Caereba Vieill.	Caereba cyanea Vieill.*
	Dacnis Cuv.	Sylvia cyanocephala Lath.*
Melithreptus Vieill.	Psophodes Vig. Horsf.	Psophodes crepitans Eyton Mag. Nat. Hist. VIII. 46.
Meliphaga Levin	Phyllornis Boie	P. Mülleri Temm.*

	Subgenera.		
Genera.	Old World.	New World.	Australia and Polynesia.
Lanius L.	Lanius	Lanius (N. America).	
	Enneoctonus Boie	Cyclorhis Sw.	
	Laniarius V.	Vireo V.	
	Telophonus Sw.		
Barita Cuv.	. . . .	. . . .	Gymnorhina Gr.
Pardalotus Vieill.	Prionochilus Strickl.		
Dicrurus V.	Dicrurus		
Campephaga V.	Campephaga		
Turdus L.	Merula Boie	Mimus B.	
	Turdus L.	Turdus L.	
	Petrocossyphus B.	Sciurus Sw.	
	Crateropus Sw.		
	Ixos T.		
Sturnus L.	Sturnus L.	Quiscalus V.	
	Dilophus V.	Sturnella V.	
	Eulabes Cuv.	Scolecophagus Sw.	
	Lamprotornis T.		
Muscicapa L.	Muscicapa Sw.		
	Muscipeta Sw.		
	Platystera J. S.		
Corvus L.	Corvus C.	Corvus (N. America).	
	Pica C.	Pica (N. America).	
		Cyanocorax Boie	
	Garrulus C.	Perisoreus Bonap.	
Bombycilla Br.	Bombycilla Br.	Bombycilla Br.	
Oriolus L.	Oriolus L.		
Cassicus Cuv.	. . . .	Cassicus C.	
		Yphantes V.	
		Icterus C.	

GENERA.	SUBGENERA.		Australia and Polynesia.
	Old World.	New World.	
		Xanthornus C.	
		Chrysomus Sw.	
		Agelaius V.	
		Molothrus Sw.	
		Dolichonyx Sw.	
Fringilla L.	*Coccothraustes* Br.	*Coccothraustes* Br.	
	Pyrgita C.	*Niphaea* Audub.	
	Fringilla Sw.	*Passerella* Sw.	
	Carduelis Briss.		
	Estrelda Sw.	*Zonotrichia* Sw.	
	Cannabina Brehm	*Coturniculus* Bonap.	
	Amadina Sw.	*Ammodramus* Sw.	
	Textor T.	*Spizella* Bonap.	
	Chrysomitris Boie	*Chrysomitris* B.	
	Erythrospiza Bonap.	*Erythrospiza* Bonap.	
	Linaria Bechst.	*Linaria* B.	
	Crithagra Sw.	*Spiza* Bonap.	
	Emberiza L.		
	Corythus C.	*Corythus* C.	
	Plectrophanes M.	*Plectrophanes* M.	
	Pyrrhula C.		
	Ploceus C.	*Coccoborus* Briss.	
	Ligurinus Br.		
	Euplectes Sw.		
	Vidua C.		
	Loxia L.	*Loxia* L.	
Tanagra L.	. . . .	*Tanagra* L.	
		Bethylus Cuv.	
		Calospiza Gr.	
		Saltator V.	
		Rhamphopsis V.	
		Tachyphonus V.	
		Pyranga V.	
		Tanagrella Sw.	
		Arremon Vieill.	
		Euphone Desm.	
		Pipilo V.	
		Procnopis Cab.	
		Icteria V.	
Motacilla L.	*Zosterops* Vig.	*Myiodioctes* Audub.	
	Phyllopneuste	*Sialia* Sw.	
	Dandalus Boie	*Trichas* Sw.	
	Hippolais Brehm	*Sylvicola* Sw.	

GENERA.	SUBGENERA.		
	Old World.	New World.	Australia and Polynesia.
	Saxicola Bechst.	*Culicivora* Sw.	
	Curruca Bechst.		
	Prinia Horsf.	*Vermivora* Sw.	
	Regulus Ray	*Regulus* R.	
	Jora Horsf.		
	Accentor Bechst.		
	Orthothomus Horsf.		
	Troglodytes Koch	*Troglodytes* K.	
		Thriothorus V.	
		Campylorhynchus Spix.	
	Anthus Bechst.	*Anthus* B.	
	Motacilla Bechst.		
Parus L.	*Parus* L.	*Parus* L.	
	Calamophilus Leach		
Timalia Horsf.	*Timalia* Horsf.		
Cinclus Bechst.	*Cinclus* Bechst.	*Cinclus*.	
Hirundo Cuv.	*Chelidon* Boie	*Chelidon* B.	
	Cotile B.	*Cotile* B.	
		Progne B.	
Alauda L.	*Alauda* L.		
	Macronyx Sw.		
	Otocoris Bonap.	*Otocoris*.	
Certhia L.	*Certhia* L.	*Certhia*.	
Sitta L.	*Sitta* L.	*Sitta* L.	
Nectarinia Ill.	*Nectarinia* Ill.	. . . .	*Drepanis* T.
	Arachnothera Temm.		
	Dicaeum Cuv.	. . . .	*Dicaeum*.
Caereba V.	. . . .	*Certhiola* Sund.	
		Caereba V.	
		Dacnis Cuv.	
Melithreptus V.	. . . .	. . . .	*Psophodes* V. H.
Meliphaga Levin	*Phyllornis* Boie		

IV. Account of Observed Forms of Larynx.

(i.) Organ of Voice of *Chasmarhynchus*.

That the lower larynx of *Chasmarhynchus* is very muscular has been long known from a remark of Prince Max von Wied[1], and from the figure which he gave of the larynx of *Chasmarhynchus nudicollis* Spix. At first one only recognises from the figure that the lower larynx has a very highly muscular covering, but it is uncertain whether the organ is formed on the type of the so-called muscular organ of voice or not. These birds are remarkable for their harmonious voice, which Prince Max compares to the tone of a clear-sounding bell; it is uttered once, lasts a long time, and is generally repeated again soon, just as if a smith repeatedly struck his anvil. Marcgrav made a very similar comparison as to the voice of the Guirapunga, *C. variegatus*: Duplicem autem sonum edit promiscue, una vice quasi quis securi percuteret cuneum ferreum in silva (*cock, cick*), altera autem quasi quis campanam fissam tangeret *kur, kur, kur*, cet[2]. According to Rich. Schomburgk, whose observations were made on *C. carunculatus*, the tones are modulated also; consequently the mechanism must be carefully studied. I examined two of the examples sent home by Schomburgk in spirit of *C. carunculatus*, and two larynges sent by Sello, with the trachea and tongue of another species, probably *C. nudicollis*, as the form of the organ quite agrees with the figure of the same given by Prince Max. These two larynges I found, with other unnamed material sent by Sello, in the stores of the Anatomical Museum, and they struck me at once by their extraordinary covering of muscle, which holds the same relation to the larynx of the Singing Birds, as the muscular stomach of a Fowl to that of the Singing Birds. I was long unable to make out from what bird this marvellous larynx came, but when I examined the *Chasmarhynchus* sent home by Schomburgk, the matter was at once clear. These larynges of Sello agree in all essential points, exactly, with the larynx of *C. carunculatus*, and with no other bird; they are only more muscular, and consequently differ in the arrangement of the vocal bands. The examination also of the trachea, tongue, and mucous membrane of the mouth, rendered the agreement more remarkable, namely, in the exactly similar tongue, in the trachea which anteriorly is wide, and gradually narrows, and in the blackish colour of the mucous membrane of the mouth. By the assistance of the figure of Prince Max the larynges of Sello can be

---

[1] Beiträge zur Naturgeschichte von Brasilien. B. III.
[2] Hist. nat. Brasiliae, Lugd. B. 1648, p. 202.

ascribed to *Chasmarhynchus nudicollis*, by which name I shall henceforward designate them.

Chasmarhynchus carunculatus. The whole larynx is surrounded, on all sides, by a thick layer of muscle, which forms, with the larynx lying beneath, two large balls, united together. Moreover, on the lower surface of the *pessulus* lies muscle, which covers the greater part of it. But the enormous mass of muscle, which is provided with a very thick nerve (a branch of the *vagus*), is not divided into separate muscles, as in the so-called muscular organ of voice, but nearly all the bundles of muscle form a united inseparable whole, of which only a right and left moiety are distinguishable, perfectly close to each other anteriorly, as well as posteriorly. All the fibres, anteriorly, laterally, and posteriorly, have a similar course from above downwards. Very peculiar and unexampled is, also, the fact that a great, and indeed the greatest portion, of the muscle is not arranged for the movement of the bronchial rings, but is inserted, between the lower edge of the larynx and the first half-ring, into the mucous membrane, while the muscular fibres, rising in the form of a bow, are set with their ends perpendicular to the mucous membrane. Thus there is formed a thick cushion-like muscular labium, on the outer wall of the organ of voice, at the entrance of each bronchus. See the section, Plate I, Fig. 7. The cushion-like labium has, on its inner aspect, opposite the cavity of the organ of voice, two surfaces, an upper larger and a lower smaller, which turn towards the first half-ring; on the edge, where the two surfaces meet, there lies an elastic strap, the outer vocal band. The muscular mass of the labium forms the thick deeper portion of the muscular covering. The superficial part of the covering, which is in no way separated from the deeper part, causes all the bundles of muscle, which come to the labium, to be invisible, and is used for the movement of the first and second half-rings. The first half-ring is enwrapped by it in its whole breadth, the second only at its anterior and posterior ends. The second half-ring can be slightly separated from the first, which is completely hidden in the muscle: between the second and third there is a large semilunar interspace; and the following half-rings are again nearer to one another. On the anterior face, the muscle curves across the lower edge of the larynx, so as to embrace the anterior ends of the first two half-rings; on the posterior, the muscle passes over the lower edge of the larynx to go to the *membrana tympaniformis* of each bronchus, which is held in tension at the point where it is fastened to the lower edge of the larynx, or of the pessulus, by a short broad muscle—a continuation of the course just described.

The outer end of this continuation of muscles projects sharply forward into the *membrana tympaniformis*, and breaks up into elastic bundles, which lie in this thick membrane. The *membrana tympaniformis* has, further, an anterior tensor, which lies on the anterior half of the pessulus, in the lower median part of the larynx, and consists of cross bundles. They do not arise from the pessulus, but are united to it by a median tendinous strap. This cross muscle is, similarly, a continuation of the muscular layer of the anterior face of the larynx. In *Chasmarhynchus nudicollis* it is, in fact, a direct continuation of it, but in this species it appears as a separate muscle.

The *musculus sternotrachealis* arises more from the anterior than from the lateral faces, just above the covering of muscle.

Chasmarhynchus nudicollis. The organ of voice is, broadly speaking, formed in just the same way, the muscular labium is again present, and the whole arrangement of the muscular supply is on the same plan; nowhere can any separation into distinct muscles be recognised. The superficial layer of the thick muscular mass, so far as can be seen, laterally, ends in the first and second half-rings of the bronchi. The first ring is quite enveloped in muscle, the second is supplied by the external muscular bundles anteriorly and posteriorly, which are inserted not only into its ends, but, also, somewhat into its whole extent. On the anterior and posterior faces of the larynx, the bundles of muscle go to the inferior surface of the organ, between the bronchi. Those of the posterior face embrace a cartilaginous projection of the bone of the larynx, to which the first half-ring, as also the end of the first and second half-rings, is fastened. But the muscle passes forward to the pessulus; this portion of the muscle which stretches the inner vocal band, arises as much from the anterior median portion of the larynx, as from the pessulus. *C. nudicollis* has, it must be said, a very thick inner vocal band, of which there is no trace in *C. carunculatus*. This band is fastened to the hinder edge of the bone of the larynx, and superiorly it passes on to the just mentioned tensor muscle. The muscular bundles wind round this band, just like a string grasped by the fingers and the hand, and must produce a considerable tension of the elastic band. This muscle extends over half the length of the pessulus. In a vertical section of the lateral masses of the muscle of the larynx, one recognises at once the muscular outer labium, and the fine external vocal band lying on it. Here also the considerable space, between the lower edge of the larynx and the first half-ring, is occupied by a thick layer of muscle, taking its origin from the larynx, and rendered invisible by the superficial layer which belongs to the half-rings; it is directed in a curve towards the mucous membrane. In this muscular wall, where the mucous membrane receives the ends of the muscular fibres, a larger inner, and a smaller lower, layer, are distinguishable, to the edge of which the elastic strap, or external vocal band is directed.

The bell-like tones of *C. nudicollis* are doubtless partly formed by the assistance of such strong inner vocal bands. The apparatus for the tension of this band is very peculiar, and reappears in no other bird. According to Rich. Schomburgk's account *C. carunculatus* should also possess a bell-like voice. The external vocal band, found in both species on the muscular labium, and the labia themselves, which are specially able to change their form above and below the elastic strap, appear to be still more essential for the production of the voice of these animals.

(ii.) Organ of Voice of the *Piprinae*.

In *Pipra pareola*, which is more closely allied to the genus *Phoenicercus* Sw. than the other *Piprinae*, the lower larynx is very different anteriorly and posteriorly. The cartilaginous rings of the trachea abut, posteriorly, on a rhomboidal shield, which blends with them; the trachea then, anteriorly, divides, but remains for three or four rings undivided posteriorly, because these rings abut by their inner ends on the already mentioned shield. Then follow, in the bronchus, three broad half-rings, which are completed by the *membrana tympaniformis;* the succeeding half-rings are thinner. The single vocal muscle, which is extraordinarily thick, arises from the lower larynx, covers the whole of the anterior and lateral portions of the larynx, but leaves the posterior free; it ends, still broad in form, in the third half-ring. All the fibres have a similar course from above downwards. It is possible to separate three longitudinal portions in the thick muscle. The lateral muscles of the trachea pass down its sides as far as the vocal muscle. The *sternotracheales* spring from the anterior wall of the trachea, and are considerable muscles.

In the short-tailed *Piprinae*, *P. leucocilla* and *P. auricapilla* Licht. the lateral muscles of the trachea, by turning forwards, cover the lower part of the anterior wall of the trachea.

In *Pipra leucocilla*, the large lateral muscles of the trachea are continued directly into the vocal muscle of the corresponding sides, and further on pass over the beginning of the bronchi to be attached to the third bronchial ring. At the bronchus, each lateral muscle divides into two bundles, an anterior and posterior, which however are left slightly uncovered by the upper surface of the third half-ring. This ring is very large, and osseous, and indeed almost a complete ring. The first and second rings of the bronchus are perfect rings. The vocal band is fastened to the inner surface of the third or large ring. The next half-ring is easily moved, and very thin, as are those which follow.

The *musculi sternotracheales*, which are not connected with the lateral muscles of the trachea in this species of *Pipra*, are inserted into the sides of the trachea.

In *Pipra manacus* L. also, the lateral muscles of the trachea turn completely forwards, and pass directly into the laryngeal muscles of their sides; which, undivided and not narrowed, are inserted into the third, very strong, bronchial ring.

In *P. auricapilla* Licht. (Doubl. Verz. 302) which is closely allied to *P. erythrocephala*, the lower portion of the lateral muscles of the trachea, cover, moreover, its whole anterior wall; the laryngeal muscles, however, are not direct prolongations of these, but are considerable muscles, which arise, where these end, at the lower end of the trachea. They cover, as a single pretty considerable muscle, the anterior portion of the bronchus of their side, as far as the third bronchial ring; the hinder portion of the bronchus they leave free. The fibres have all the same course. The first two of the bronchial ring are perfect rings; the third is a broad osseous plate, on which the vocal muscles are fastened; the following half-rings are thin, the first sigmiform.

In *Jodopleura pipra* Lesson, the lateral muscles retain their lateral position. The laryngeal muscle moves the second bronchial ring. All the bronchial rings are only half-rings, and of very much the same form.

Calyptura cristata Sw. resembles, in its larynx, more the true *Ampelinae* than the rest of the *Piprinae*; it possesses only an extremely fine prolongation of the lateral muscle of the trachea to the bronchus, to the second ring of which it is attached. The bronchi possess no whole rings, and only the third is very moveable.

In the *membrana tympaniformis* of the *Piprinae*, there are no small cartilages, as there are in so many other birds.

The *Piprinae* were thrown by Swainson and Gray with *Pardalotus* and *Prionochilus* into one family of *Piprinae*; but these Australian and Indian genera are Singing Birds. I have examined *Prionochilus* Strickl.

(iii.) Organ of Voice of the *Ampelinae* and *Eurylaiminae*.

After removing *Bombycilla*, there belong to the *Ampelinae* the South American genera with the very simplest form of larynx, namely, *Cephalopterus* Geoffr., *Gymnocephalus* Geoffr., *Rupicola* Briss., *Phibalura* Vieill., *Cotinga* Briss., *Psaris* Cuv., *Pachyrhamphus* Gray, and some others, which I have not examined. Most of them live only on plants (berries); some, on mixed food, as *Gymnocephalus*, in whose stomach I have found berries and insects; *Psaris* and *Pachyrhamphus* on insects. All have the hinder surface of the tarsus covered with small scales. They have been thrown here and there by systematists, and disposed of in different places. Cuvier put *Psaris* with the Shrikes, Swainson and Gray with the *Muscicapidae*, and the latter put *Cephalopterus* and *Gymnocephalus* with the Corvidae. The true position of *Psaris* was very rightly perceived by Cabanis, who has made use of the examination of their vocal organ. *Phytotoma*, which has the same covering to the tarsus, is also placed by him in this family; but I have not examined this genus.

In the majority of the *Ampelinae* no considerable laryngeal muscle exists, and the lateral muscle of the trachea is simply prolonged as far as the bronchus, as in the *Coracianae*, *Upupinae*, *Caprimulginae*, most of the *Syndactyli*, and many *Scansores*.

In *Ampelis (Cotinga) pompadora* the first four rings (half-rings) of the bronchus are broad, and can, like tiles, be separated from one another; the very thin prolongation of the lateral muscle of the trachea is inserted into the fifth, which is quite narrow, as are all that follow it. In *Rupicola cayana* the thin lateral muscle is inserted into the first half-ring, which is quite small.

In *Gymnocephalus calvus* the first five half-rings are broad and flat. The thin lateral muscle raises the fourth half-ring. The upper part of the trachea presents the same spindle-shaped widening, as v. Tschudi has described in *Cephalopterus*. In *Psaris cayanus* the thin lateral muscle of the trachea extends to the second half-ring of the bronchus; after which thin half-rings follow.

The *musculi sternotracheales*[1] exist in a very large majority of the singing and screeching Passerines. The genus *Pachyrhamphus* Gray (*Pachyrhynchus* Spix), which is closely allied to *Psaris*, is strikingly distinguished from *Psaris* by its larynx; it is the only genus of the *Ampelinae* which has a large laryngeal muscle not connected with the lateral muscles of the trachea.

In *Pachyrhamphus atricapillus* Cab. (*Pipra atricapilla* Gm., *Lanius mitratus* Licht. Doubl. Verz. p. 50), the lateral muscles of the trachea finally turn forwards, and completely cover the anterior wall of the lower portion of the trachea, until they terminate at its end in a common point. The *musculi sternotracheales* must be regarded, on the whole, as independent muscles, since they generally have no connection with the lateral muscles, but arise, on the contrary, from the sides of the trachea. A peculiar laryngeal muscle arises from the end of the trachea, and is inserted into the second half-ring of the bronchus.

This condition of the lateral muscles of the trachea I have again found in a genus of the *Tyranninae*—*Pyrocephalus* Gould.

In *Phibalura flavirostris* Vieill., the elongated thin lateral muscle is inserted into the third bronchial ring.

---

[1] I have only examined the musculi sternotracheales in *Eulabes religiosa* Cuv. and in *Trochilus*, among the Passerines. Among the *Scansores* they are wanting, according to Wagner, in the *Psittacinae*.

In the *Ampelinae*, as in the *Piprinae*, the peculiar cartilages of the *membrana tympaniformis*, which are characteristic of the *Tyranninae*, are wanting. The *Eurylaiminae* of the Old World are close to the *Ampelinae*—that is, *Eurylaimus* and *Calyptomena*. I have examined *Eurylaimus corydon* Temm., the type of the genus *Corydon* Less. In this bird I remarked no muscular fibres on the larynx.

(iv.) Organ of Voice of the *Tyranninae* and *Fluvicolinae*.

The *Muscicapidae* of the New World, or *Tyrannidae*, are separated from those of the Old World, not only by the want of the highly muscular larynx, but also by external characters; their feet are covered on the hinder, or inner, side with a band of small scales, or are quite naked, while the *Muscicapidae* of the Old World possess the bilaminate tarsus of Singing Birds. Further, the *Tyrannidae* have a well developed first primary, which is completely aborted in the *Muscicapidae* of the Old World, as Swainson has already shown. In short, they are perfectly distinct families. Gray has united them in his family of the *Muscicapidae* (as Cuvier in *Muscicapa*), and in it has separated the *Tyranninae*, *Muscicapinae*, and others; but his *Muscicapinae*, as with Swainson, is a collection of South American Passerines without the muscular organ of voice, together with *Muscicapidae* of the Old World with this organ, and contains birds of three different families.

In the family of the *Tyrannidae*, the genera of the *Tyranninae* and *Fluvicolinae* offer some interesting variations from the general ground-type of larynx without complex vocal muscles. The only feature common to all the genera is the possession of a single muscle, which may be very broad and thick, as in most of the *Tyranninae* and *Fluvicolinae*, but in some it is so small, that it only appears to be a prolongation of the lateral muscle of the trachea. All have a *cartilago arytaenoidea* in the *membrana tympaniformis*, and, in most, some of the upper rings of the bronchi are perfect, so that they resemble the trachea. Some genera offer very remarkable peculiarities. One of the chief forms of those with a single thick muscle was observed by Audubon.

Saurophagus Sw., *Tyrannus* Cuv., *Tyrannula* Sw., *Elaenia* Sund., *Platyrhynchus* Desm., and in general the *Tyranninae* have a thick broad laryngeal muscle, which is not attached to the posterior face of the larynx.

In *Saurophagus sulphuratus* Sw. (*Tyrannus sulphuratus* Cuv.), the first five bronchial rings are broad and touch; the first four are not at all moveable, and indeed the first three partly blend on their outer sides. The first three bronchial rings are perfect. The muscle is inserted into the fourth, and into the hinder part of the fifth bronchial ring (half-ring).

The sixth bronchial ring is one of the true thin half-rings, and follows the movements of those before it, but the next is separated from it by the external *membrana tympaniformis*. Special vocal bands exist merely as folds of the mucous membrane on the moveable half-rings. The *cartilago arytaenoidea* in the *membrana tympaniformis* is small, with four corners, and is fastened to the third bronchial ring.

Tyrannus crudelis Sw. (*Musc. despotes* Licht.) has three perfect rings at the commencement of the bronchus. The muscle is attached to the fourth ring, but appears to move the superior rings also; it is less broad than in the previously mentioned bird.

Tyrannus ferox Cuv. (*Muscicapa ferox* Gm.), genus *Tyrannula* Sw., has only one perfect bronchial ring; the broad muscle is inserted into the next half-ring. The *cartilago arytaenoidea* in the *membrana tympaniformis* is very large, and broader at the end turned away from the division of the trachea; it projects into a lateral process, which is united to a second small cartilage by a band. The latter lies between the ends of the fourth and fifth bronchial rings.

In *Elaenia brevirostris* v. Tschudi (Wiegm. Archiv. 1844) also there is only one complete bronchial ring. The *membrana tympaniformis* contains a very considerable *cartilago arytaenoidea*. The muscle, of the same character as in the Tyranninae, is inserted into the second bronchial ring. The posterior portion of the larynx is without muscle.

In *Elaenia pagana* Sund. (*Muscicapa pagana* Licht., *Platyrhynchus paganus* Spix.) the muscle, and the *cartilago arytaenoidea* are similar; but a complete bronchial ring is wanting. The broad thick muscle is inserted into the second half-ring.

Machetornis rixosa Gray, which Herr Stannius most kindly gave me, has an unusually thin muscle, but completely agrees in the structure and muscular supply of its larynx with the rest of the *Tyrannidae*, and true species of *Tyrannus*.

In the Peruvian species of *Platyrhynchus*, which could not be exactly named on account of the incomplete supply of its feathers, there are two or three perfect bronchial rings. The muscle, as in *Tyrannus* and *Elaenia*, does not touch the hinder portion of the larynx, and is inserted without contracting into the first, slightly moveable, half-ring.

The genus *Pyrocephalus* Gould., *P. coronatus* G. (*Muscicapa coronata* L. Gm.) differs from the foregoing *Tyranninae*. In it the lateral muscles of the trachea turn towards its anterior wall, in the lower part of the trachea, while they terminate in a common point at its end, as in *Pachyrhamphus* among the *Ampelinae*. The first of the bronchial rings is perfect. The muscles for the movement of the bronchial rings are reduced to a minimum; a scarcely recognisable remnant of muscle goes from the last tracheal, to the anterior edge of the second bronchial, ring. The *cartilago arytaenoidea* is present.

In *Myiobius* Gray, and *Arundinicola* D'Orb. Lafr., no large laryngeal muscles exist; the lateral muscle of the trachea is simply prolonged to the bronchi. In *Myiobius erythrurus* Mus. Berol., the first two bronchial rings are perfect, and the muscle raises the third; in *Arundinicola leucocephala* (*Todus leucocephalus* Gm.) no bronchial ring is perfect; the slight prolongation of the lateral muscle is inserted into the second bronchial ring. The *cartilago arytaenoidea* is present.

In the *Fluvicolae* examined by me, the lower portion of the trachea was quite covered by the lateral muscles on its anterior wall; though not ending in a point, they terminate where the broad laryngeal muscles arise, which latter perfectly resemble the same muscles in the *Tyranninae*, and end, without contracting, on one of the bronchial rings. The posterior portion of the larynx is not covered by the muscle.

In *Fluvicola* (*Entomophagus*) *bicolor* (*Muscicapa bicolor* L. Gm., *M. albiventris* Spix) no perfect bronchial ring exists. The muscle is inserted into the first half-ring. The *cartilago arytaenoidea* of the *membrana tympaniformis* is semilunar.

The genus *Centrites* Cabanis belongs to the *Fluvicolinae*, of which *Alauda rufa* Gm. is the type. Tracheal and laryngeal muscles, as in the preceding; the first bronchial ring is perfect. There is a *cartilago arytaenoidea*.

(v.) Organ of Voice of the *Todinae* and *Platyrhynchinae*, Cab.

Some of the Todus-like *Tyrannidae* differ very greatly from the type of this family, not only in the want of the perfect rings in the bronchi, and their flattened commencement, but also in the absence of the *cartilago arytaenoidea* in the *membrana tympaniformis*. To such belongs the new genus *Colopterus* Cabanis, for example, which is characterised and easily known by the first three or four primaries being much shorter than the rest. Our Museums here possess two species of this genus, which have been described by Cabanis in the Archiv für Naturgeschichte. The species which I examined, *Colopterus cristatus* Cab., from Guiana, had the first three primaries short. In this small bird the last twelve rings of the trachea are laterally compressed. It is still more remarkable that these twelve rings are cleft completely behind, and that a small bony clasp, which is connected with the pessulus of the tracheal portion, is placed between the ends of the cleft rings. Not one of the bronchial rings is perfect. The first four half-rings are very broad; into the fourth the not very broad muscle is inserted; this descends obliquely from before backwards, and ends in a point. A perfectly peculiar muscle is a large azygos one, which shortens the compressed lower portion of the trachea, and reaches as far as the last tracheal ring and the pessulus. The lateral muscles of the trachea, and the *musculi sternotrachealos* are of the ordinary form.

A genus allied to this has been discovered, which also stands very close to it in regard to the larynx—the genus *Orchilus* Cab. (*Todus megacephalus* Sw.) The five lowest rings of the trachea are cleft behind, and contain in this cleft a small bony clasp, which is a continuation of the pessulus. The laryngeal muscle resembles that of *Colopterus* in direction, and is inserted into the hinder part of the fourth half-ring. The azygos muscle of the trachea, found in *Colopterus*, is wanting.

Another genus of the *Todinae*, *Todirostrum* Less. (*Triccus* Cab.) wants the cleft. It has no large laryngeal muscle, but the lateral muscle of the trachea is simply continued to the bronchus, and raises the fourth half-ring, as in *Myiobius* and *Arundinicola*. The *cartilago ayrtaenoidea* is wanting; the branches of the trachea resemble those of the rest of the *Todinae*. I have examined *Todirostrum cinereum* Less. (*Todus cinereus* L.) and *Triccus poliocephalus* Cab. (*Todus poliocephalus* Pr. M.)

These four species of the *Todinae* examined by me possess only a single notch in the sternum. The type of the true genus *Todus*, *T. viridis* L. has two notches on each side. The trachea is perfect; I cannot say how the tracheal muscle is situated, on account of the imperfect state of the birds examined.

(vi.) Organ of Voice of the *Myiotherinae*, *Scytalopinae*, *Anabatinae*, and *Dendrocolaptinae*.

In most birds the organ of voice is formed by the end of the trachea and the beginning of the bronchi. In some it is altogether bronchial, as is the case in *Steatornis* and *Crotophaga*. In *S. caripensis* the bronchi preserve, for a long distance, the perfect rings of the trachea, so that there are from eleven to sixteen perfect bronchial rings; the next ring is very strong and no longer perfect, the following half-ring is still thicker, and is acted on by the vocal muscle. In *C. major* there are eight perfect bronchial rings, and the muscle is inserted into the tenth.

A division of the Passerines, which is partly placed under the Shrikes, partly under the Thrushes, partly under the Fly-catchers, and partly under the Wrens, is distinct among birds from the peculiarity, till now unknown, that the organ of voice is formed by the lower larynx alone without the aid of the bronchi; and this offers a perfectly aberrant form of structure. This portion of the trachea is flattened from before backwards, its walls are thin and membranous, and consists of extremely fine anterior and posterior half-rings, which are fastened to the sides by long elastic bands. The position of these half-rings is altered by the muscles fastened to their sides. In all these birds the cartilaginous pessulus in the furcation of the trachea is wanting, and is replaced by a tendinous strap. The *membrana tympaniformis* passes over from one bronchus to the other. The bronchi consist of half-rings only. The membranous wall of the organ of voice consists of two thin transparent membranes, of which the inner is the mucous membrane.

This structure is found in the genera *Thamnophilus* Vieill., *Myiothera* Ill., *Conopophaga* Vieill., *Chamaeza* Vig., *Scytalopus* Gould, *Tinactor* Pr. M., *Furnarius* Vieill., *Cinclodes* Gray, *Anabates* Temm., *Synallaxis* Vieill., *Xenops* Hoffm., *Dendrocolaptes* Herm., and their allies.

Thamnophilus. The normal strong rings of the trachea cease before the furcation, and that suddenly; there is only one strong tracheal ring at the furcation, with which the bronchi are connected. In the intervening portion, the trachea is membranous and transparent, and this voice-forming portion of the trachea, or, as we would call it, the vocal membrane, consists generally of six, and seldom of fewer, extremely fine tracheal rings of extraordinary tenuity, so that they appear as lines to the naked eye. They are however ossified. The rings are soft and intercepted at the sides, and are held together by an elastic longitudinal band which extends to the last ring of the trachea. All this region of the trachea is very strongly flattened from before backwards. In *Thamnophilus guttatus* the lowest portion of the trachea is also remarkably flattened. The voice is produced by the vibrations of the half-rings, and of the thin membranous interspaces. The voice-producing portion of the trachea is contracted by a muscle on either side, which arises from the lower large rings of the trachea, and is attached to the whole length of the band which holds together the half-rings, and finally to the last ring, which is again perfect, but not to the bronchi. The half-rings of the bronchi are in no way peculiar.

Again, it is remarkable as regards the genus *Thamnophilus*, that in all the species of it that I have examined, the ordinary depressor of the trachea, or *sternotrachealis* has two heads; the stronger being attached to the firm portion of the trachea above the tracheal organ of voice, the thinner, which is inferior, to the side of the lower portion of the membranous division of the trachea, by the lateral band, close behind the proper muscle of the larynx, at the spot where the band unites the last pair of their half-rings. This head is united to the upper depressor, and both pass outwards and downwards to form the *sternotrachealis*. See Pl. II. *Thamnophilus naevius* (*Lanius naevius* L. Gm.), *Thamnophilus guttatus* Spix. (*Lanius meleager* Licht. Doubl. Verz. 491), *Thamnophilus cristatus* Pr. M., *Thamnophilus doliatus* (*Lanius doliatus* L.) have been examined.

Vieillot, who first separated this genus from *Lanius*, left it in the family of Shrikes, *Colluriones*; Cuvier never recognised the difference between them and *Lanius*, and consequently put the *Thamnophili*, again, as species of the genus *Lanius*, in the strict sense. Swainson united *Thamnophilus* with some of the genus *Lanius* of the Old World in a false sub-family *Thamnophilinae*, in the family *Laniadae*, and in this Gray has followed him. Prince Max von Neuwied is the only one who recognised the natural position of this bird. According to him *Thamnophilus* has not the mode of life of *Lanius*, but principally that of the *Myiotherae*, living not on the ground, but on branches of trees. According to the same observer they are solitary peaceful birds, with a voice, in some loud and very remarkable, and in others loud, but ordinary.

Myiothera Ill. The organ of voice of *Myiothera* agrees exactly with that of *Thamnophilus*, in the vibrating half-rings of the trachea, as well as in the lateral bands, and the tracheal muscle; the single difference lies in the peculiarity of the *musculus sternotrachealis*, which has not two heads, as in *Thamnophilus*, but arises from the strong portion of the trachea. I examined *M. margaritacea* Licht. Mus. Berol. (*Turdus tintinnabulatus* Gm.)

The genera *Thamnophilus* and *Myiothera* are very closely related, both in external and in internal characters, and belong to the same family *Myiotherinae*, to which, in our sense, only birds of the New World at present belong; the two genera are however very distinct in the covering of the foot, which has in *Thamnophilus* two series of large plates on its posterior face.

Conopophaga Vieill. *Conopophaga* stands nearest to the preceding genera; the flat membranous portion of the trachea with fine vibrating half-rings and lateral bands, is again present, but the first two bronchial half-rings, while uniting with one another, and with the last tracheal ring, begin to be more strongly developed. These two great half-rings consequently lose their ordinary connection with the bronchi, and form the lower limit of the tracheal organ of voice: the first half-ring of each bronchus is also raised in a pyramidal manner, as we shall see still more markedly in the following genera.

Conopophaga aurita Vieill. has six fine vibrating half-rings of the membranous portion of the trachea; it is the only genus of the family in which I have found no true laryngeal muscle. The *musculus sternotrachealis* arises from the end of the firm part of the trachea.

Vieillot, Cuvier, Swainson, and Gray placed this genus with the Fly-catchers.

Chamaeza Vig. The first two rings of the bronchi are in this bird as large, and as united as in *Conopophaga*; on the upper one there is placed a long sharply-ending cartilage, which rises up at the sides of the tracheal organ of voice. It is the muscular process of the bronchi, or what here will henceforward be called the *processus vocalis* of the tracheophone larynx. It is not in close relation with the vibrating portion of the trachea, but lies free on its sides; to its sharp end, which reaches as far as the upper end of the tracheal larynx, is attached the end of the lateral muscle of the trachea, and when these muscles are in action and pull on the *processus vocales* of the bronchi, the membranous portion of the trachea is contracted, and the numerous fine vibrating half-rings are brought close together. The *musculi sternotracheales* arise in this genus, and in all that follow, not from the trachea, but from the points of the *processus vocales*[1]. In the membranous portion of the trachea, there are, in both its anterior and posterior flattened walls, very many fine half-rings. The three lowest are somewhat stronger and are in connection with the *processus vocales*, the succeeding half-rings vibrate, and the ends of these half-rings are inserted into the lateral bands of the membranous portion of the trachea. In all, the membranous portion of the trachea has thirteen fine thin half-rings in its anterior wall, and a similar number in its posterior.

Species examined *Chamaeza meruloides* Vig.

Grallaria Vieill. also belongs, without doubt, to this group, which is only separated from *Chamaeza* by the absence of plates on the hinder side of the foot. I have not, however, examined *Grallaria*.

Scytalopus Gould. This genus also has the high pyramidal *processus vocales* on the first bronchial rings, from the points of which the *musculi sternotracheales* arise, and which are drawn up to the strong rings of the trachea by other muscles. The vibrating half-rings of the trachea are of the form common in this family. I examined *Scytalopus indigoticus* (*Myiothera indigotica* Pr. M.).

This genus, which is closely allied to *Pteroptochus*, is with *Pteroptochus*, distinguished from all previously mentioned, and all succeeding genera which possess the tracheal larynx, by the two deep notches on either side of the sternum; and since the feet of *Scytalopus* and *Pteroptochus* are covered with two series of large plates on the hinder surface (as in *Thamnophilus* and *Chamaeza*), it is probable that *Pteroptochus* also possesses the same tracheal larynx, and so it can with great probability be placed in this family, although Eyton's anatomical note on *P. tarnii* does not allow us to form any conclusions as to the existence of any tracheal larynx.

---

[1] An instance, as observed by me in many other birds, that the *musculus sternotrachealis* is not produced to the sides of the trachea (Cuvier), but rather that the lateral muscles of the trachea and the *sternotracheales* are different muscles.

Furnarius Vieill. (*Opetiorhynchus* Temm., *Figulus* Spix.) The first and second half-rings of the bronchi are united to one another, to form the lateral bases of the tracheal larynx. These lateral bases are connected by one anterior and one posterior strip of cartilage; on the posterior face a bent cartilage is placed, in the furcation of the trachea, between the two bronchi. On the first bronchial ring a long osseous pyramid is so placed, that its base reaches to the second half-ring of the bronchus. This bone extends upwards, free, on the sides of the membranous portion of the trachea, as far as the region of its firm portion. The *processus vocalis* is only connected to the trachea by the muscles, which arise from the latter, and are fastened to the former. *Furnarius* has two such muscles on either side, one anterior and one posterior; and the position of them is the same in all the succeeding genera. These muscles arise from the lower portion of the trachea, and are attached to the anterior and posterior edges of the *processus vocalis* nearer its base. From its tip arises the *musculus sternotrachealis*. The membranous portion of the trachea, in the tracheal organ of voice, again consists of the transparent membranes of the larynx, and the extremely fine, and linear, though osseous anterior and posterior half-rings, which are contained in its flat membranous walls. These are only half-rings, and their ends are connected to the sides by the elastic band, which reaches from the trachea to the bronchus. There are six or seven such half-rings in the anterior and posterior walls. The membranous portion of the trachea is contracted, and the vibrating half-rings brought closer together, when the two muscles on either side of the *processus vocalis*, and consequently the bronchi, and the lower end of the trachea, are raised. The *musculi sternotracheales* produce the opposite result.

I examined *Furnarius rufus* Vieill. (*Turdus badius* Licht. Doubl. Verz. 441) and *F. leucopus* Sw.

The genus *Cinclodes* Gray (*Cillurus* Cab.) is similar. I examined *Cillurus nigrofumosus* Cab. in v. Tschudi in Wiegm. Archiv. 1844 (*Upucerthia nigrofumosa* D'Orb.).

So too the genus *Anabates*. I examined *A. contaminatus* Mus. Berol., *A. adspersus* M. B., *A. albicollis* M. B.

The base of the larynx consists of the last tracheal ring, which is cleft anteriorly, and the commencement, i.e. the first and second half-rings, of the bronchi. On the hinder face there is a large cartilage uniting the bronchi, as in *Furnarius*, and a similar smaller one anteriorly, which fills up the cleft in the last tracheal ring. The six vibrating and extremely fine half-rings of the vocal membrane of the trachea have at their sides a large but membranous gap, and in it are wanting those bands, which unite the ends of them, as in *Xenops*. The muscles of the *processus vocalis* resemble those of *Furnarius*.

Genus *Tinactor* Pr. M. The base of the tracheal larynx is formed, on either side, by the first and second bronchial half-rings, and in the middle by the lowest ring of the trachea, which is connected with it; this is complete posteriorly, but is cleft anteriorly, so that it is, in front, like a bronchial half-ring. In the membranous flattened wall of the tracheal vocal membrane there are eight extremely fine anterior and posterior half-rings. The bony piece has its base resting on the first bronchial half-ring, and the last tracheal ring. The muscles of it are double, as in *Furnarius* and *Cinclodes*.

Pr. Max was right in thinking that this bird would connect the *Myiotherae* with the *Dendrocolaptinae*.

Xenops. The base of the tracheal organ of voice is formed of the first three bronchial half-rings, which are closely connected together, and the last complete tracheal ring. The osseous pieces are as usual attached to the bronchi, and are very broad; their muscles are attached close to their tips, whence arise the *musculi sternotracheales*. The membranous portion of the trachea is longer than it is broad; it contains, however, only three extremely fine half-rings, which are embedded in the membranous wall, and never reach to the sides. I examined *Xenops rutilus* Licht.

Synallaxis Vieill. The osseous pieces are as usual, and are attached to the first and second bronchial half-rings. The base of the tracheal larynx also consists of three closely approximated and complete tracheal rings. The membranous portion of the trachea is broader than it is long, and seems to contain, at the most, a trace of half-rings; at least, in *Synallaxis ruficauda* Spix., I only noticed a single minute band, in the lower part of the membrane. The muscles of these pieces are attached to their median part.

Dendrocolaptes Herm. The base of the tracheal larynx forms two halves, one anterior and one posterior, which touch one another; the commencement of the bronchi, which are greatly enlarged, consist of the large first and second bronchial rings. On this base the pyramids or *processus vocales* are placed, which in this genus are remarkable from their sending out anteriorly and posteriorly a *processus muscularis*, which forms, as it were, a handle for the attachment of the anterior and posterior vocal muscles, which arise from the trachea. The vocal membrane of the trachea contains six to seven half-rings. The handles on the *processus vocales* resemble those in the subgenera of the *Dendrocolaptinae*. I examined *D. cayennensis* Licht., and *D. tenuirostris* Mus. Berol.

The birds with a tracheal organ of voice, which I shall henceforward merely call *Tracheophones*, are famous for their marvellous voices. Azara already has called the voice of the *Batara* (*Thamnophilus*) marvellous and strong; it consists in the continual repetition of the syllable *ta*, and can be heard half a mile off[1]. Prince Max speaks of the simple but marvellous voice of a *Thamnophilus;* the same author calls the voice of *Furnarius* very loud, and marvellous, although composed of few tones. Darwin mentions the peculiarly shrill, rapidly repeated voice of *Furnarius*[2]. According to Azara the voice of the Oven-Bird is heard half a mile off[3]. According to Swainson *Synallaxis* has a loud, and very unpleasant voice. Prince Max mentions the fine high tones of *Tinactor*, Darwin the loud cry of *Scytalopus magellanicus*[4], and the strange barking tones of *Pteroptochus*[5]. According to Kittlitz, the tones of *Pteroptochus paradoxus* are very high, more like the voice of a frog than that of a bird. Prince Max calls the voice of *Anabates erythrophthalmus* loud and marvellous.

Grallaria tinniens (*Turdus tinniens* L.) is famous for its bell-like voice; this statement of Vieillot and Buffon arises perhaps from some mistake, for no later observer has confirmed it. Moreover, one cannot expect a voluminous voice in any bird with a tracheophone vocal organ, for no means of producing it are present in this structure. I have never found large vocal bands, although I have continually made sections of this larynx; their vocal capacity is reduced to the mere vibrations of the membranous portion of the trachea, the walls of which are thrown into folds by the action of their muscles, and set in vibration by the stream of air.

All the *Tracheophones* form together one large family, and break up, in it, into several groups. All are distinguished by short rounded feathers, some by long feet, some by short tails. The extremes, *Thamnophilus* and *Dendrocolaptes*, are considerably different, although they are completely united by intermediate steps; the stiff and long shafts of the tail feathers of *Dendrocolaptes* are arrived at step by step, through the genera, *Synallaxis*, *Anabates*, and *Tinactor*.

This family with its subgenera contains, as yet, only South American forms. Further examination is needed to show whether the *Orthonyx* Temm. of New Zealand is connected with the American *Dendrocolapdae* or no. The East Indian *Myiophonus*, *Timalia*, and so-called Ant-Birds of the Old World are not allied to the *Myiotherae* of the New, and belong rather to the Singing Birds.

---

[1] Apuntiamentos, II. p. 186.　　[2] Zool. of H.M.S. Beagle, III. 64, 65.
[3] Loc. cit., II. p. 223.　　[4] Loc. cit., III. p. 72.
[5] Darwin Naturwissenschaftl. Reisen II. 22, 23, 45.

The union of *Cinclus* with the South American birds by Swainson and Gray is wrong. *Cinclus* has a complex muscular organ of voice, which I also found in the genus *Timalia* Horsf. among the before-mentioned genera.

(vii.) Organ of Voice of *Trochilus*.

The larynx, lying in the neck of the Humming Bird, which does not possess *musculi sternotracheales*, has been already examined by Meckel, Audubon, and others, but its structure has not been correctly recognised by any of these observers. The organ is thus arranged in the various subgenera of *Trochilus*, viz. *Campylopterus, Phaëtornis, Lampornis, Orthorhynchus*, and *Ornismyia :—*it possesses two muscles very peculiarly broken up; the first half-ring of the bronchus is excessively small, and inserted between the ends of the second large half-ring and the lower larynx; the ends of the second half-ring are fastened to the larynx itself, their posterior extremities are very large, and triangular; two sides of the triangle receive the muscle which, arising from the larynx anteriorly, below the middle line, passes obliquely outwards, and then bends backwards and downwards; from this end of the second half-ring arises a second muscle, which has hitherto escaped notice; this goes in an opposite direction forwards and downwards, and is inserted in the two following rings and the third, which, as all that follow it, is a perfect ring. The small *membrana tympaniformis* possesses a rounded cartilage.

(viii.) Organ of Voice of *Colius*.

Among the Passerines of the Old World, which do not possess the complex muscular organ of voice, this genus is, as far as is yet known, the only one whose larynx is peculiar. It possesses a thick vocal muscle, and is peculiar from the fact that the first bronchial ring forms an osseous triangular shield over the second and third. Into this shield is inserted the muscle, which, however, also gives off smaller branches to the anterior part of the second and third half-rings. The vocal band lies on the upper edge of the first half-ring, which is completely osseous. I have examined *C. capensis* and *C. quiriwa* Less.

It has often been lamented that the anatomy of birds is so uniform, that the labours of Zoologists receive but little assistance from their anatomy. This remark is very true; but it must be borne in mind that it is not true for all parts. The organ of voice is an exception; there are in it important characters, distinguishing genera and families, which seem, in every external character, to pass into one another. And if nature shows us in it a marvellous abundance of variations, we may compare it with the sexual parts, as shown in the examination of the Struthious Birds which I laid before the Academy in 1836.

V. ON THE RELATIONS BETWEEN THE STRUCTURE OF THE ORGAN OF VOICE, AND THE EXTERNAL CHARACTERS OF THE PASSERINES.

If we put aside the chief peculiarities of the genera, and review the most ordinary types of the larynx in the Passerines, including the Scansores, or rather the Insessores, we find that there are three chief forms of vocal organs to be examined: (1) the highly muscular larynx with anterior and posterior muscles, as found in the Songsters, *Passerini Polymyodi* (which sing with many muscles); (2) the tracheal organ of voice of the *Tracheophoni* with one or two lateral muscles; (3) the larynx of the *Picarii* with one or several lateral muscles. I do not use the names *Polymyodi, Tracheophoni, Picarii,* to distinguish divisions of the Insessores, but only provisionally for forms of the larynx. The essential point of difference between *Polymyodi* and *Picarii* is not to be regarded as lying in the different number of muscles which are present, for there are intermediate steps in this, and indeed four or five muscles on either side of the larynx, as in the Singing Birds, or three, as in the *Psittacidae,* are not very different; but the characteristic of the larynx, of the *Polymyodi* is that the influence of their muscles is divided, and is exerted on both the anterior and posterior ends of the moveable rings of the bronchi, while in the *Picarii* they only act on one part of the ring, the extent of which may vary, and may indeed be over the greater part of the breadth of one ring, as in *Tyrannus, Fluvicola,* and *Pipra.* From this point of view the larynx of *Maenura,* although it differs from that of the Songsters in the number of muscles, would be still placed in the general type of the *Polymyodi,* in so far as that the muscles act symmetrically on the ends of the half-rings. The larynx of the *Picarii* is not necessarily limited to one laryngeal muscle, but may possess several, as in the *Trochilinae,* and *Psittacinae,* but they then lie in the same plane, either over or under one another, and are not, as in the Songsters, separated into those on the anterior and those on the posterior face of the larynx. A maximum and minimum is as possible in the larynx of the *Picarii,* as in that of the Songsters; a minimum is found in the *Maenurinae,* which according to Eyton possess only an anterior and posterior laryngeal muscle, which, however, act on several rings. Several rings of the bronchi may be moved in both forms; for example, among the *Picarii*, in *Trochilus* and *Colius*, and even in some *Tyrannidae*.

On account of *Chasmarhynchus*, the exact separation of these forms of larynx becomes very hazardous, and almost impossible. For although these birds are evidently closely allied to the *Ampelinae*, and eminently resemble them in the posterior covering of elliptical scales, their larynx presents a combination of the peculiarities of the Singing Birds and of the *Picarii*; while, on the one hand, their muscular supply is more developed than it is in the Singing Birds, on the other it is not separated into different muscles, but yet it moves several half-rings; embraces the first in its whole breadth, the second at its extremities only, and acts on the latter just as do the muscles of the Singing Birds, being distributed to the anterior and posterior ends of the half rings. *Chasmarhynchus* therefore might be just as well placed among the Singing, as the Shrieking Birds. The question now arises, whether there are other characters in the external structure of the birds, which can serve as a sure sign of internal differences, and which can lead us, on account of their non-variability to understand Nature, where she leaves us in doubt as to the real bearing of the internal structure.

A difference, to which Count Keyserling and Professor Blasius first drew attention, in Wiegmann's Archiv. 1839, I. 332, appears to be of considerable importance in this matter. According to them, the foot of all birds provided with the so-called muscular organ of voice, is clothed posteriorly with a large horny covering—this is the so-called tarsal space (bilaminate planta)—or the foot of these birds is covered on its hinder surface with oblique plates as in the Larks (with which also *Maenura* would be included, if its larynx can be placed with the vocal larynx, since it has two series of plates on the hinder part of the foot). In birds without the muscular organ of voice, or the *Picarii* of Nitzsch, the foot according to the same observers, is always without the corresponding horny covering, or even the oblique plates of the Larks, and is covered with scales, reticulated, or naked.

The importance of this character has been contested by Burmeister, in Wiegm. Archiv. 1840, 220, on the ground that in many Singing Birds the posterior parts of the foot are either covered with scales, or granules, or are naked; as the *Ampelidae, Coracina, Cephalopterus, Chasmarhynchus, Ampelis, Eurylaimus, Rupicola, Pipra, Phibalura, Tyrannus,* and *Psaris*.

Blasius and Keyserling (Id. 1840, 362) do not regard these exceptions as affecting the question, for they do not regard the *Ampelidae* as Singing Birds, and see no reason why they should be so; they say that the position of *Psaris* is doubtful, and that the tarsal covering of the *Tyrannidae* differs from that of the Climbing Birds (Klettervögel)[1].

Since the *Ampelidae, Tyranni, Pipra*e, and *Psaris* do not possess a vocal larynx, as has been already described, the views of Blasius and Keyserling are so far supported. *Chasmarhynchus* on the contrary has more muscle on its larynx than any other Singing Bird, but this case alone is not decisive, because of the peculiarity of this organ. In all these birds the anterior series of tarsal plates reaches so far back on both sides, that only an exceedingly small space is generally left; this is either covered with granules or scales, or is naked. But in birds with a vocal larynx there are, ordinarily, only two posterolateral scutes, which would then form the essential point of difference, if there is present on the posterior surface of the tarsus a layer of granules between these scutes, as in *Lanius bakbakiri* and *Eulabes religiosa*; in which latter the tarsal scutes are also divided from the anterior plates by granules.

So far the *Picarii* really appear to be defined by external characters, and we seem to be able to conclude from the presence of the tarsal scutes behind the anterior plates that the muscular vocal larynx is present, and from the extension of the anterior plates to the posterior granulated or naked part, that the larynx of the *Picarii* is present.

But yet there are exceptions; the genus *Lipaugus* Boie. In *L. plumbeus* (*Muscicapa plumbea* Licht.) the hinder space is granulated, but one other very similar species of the genus, *L. calcaratus* (*Tyrannula calcarata* Sw.) has a series of plates on the outer posterior side of the foot, and the inner posterior side is naked. The genus *Gubernetes* of the family of *Fluvicolinae* (with spots on the wings, as the other *Fluvicolinae*) has, on the posterior part of the foot, two series of plates. The genera *Setophaga, Myiobius, Arundinicola* (*Todus leucocephalus* Gm.), and *Celopterus* Cab. are not Singing Birds, but belong, according to the structure of their larynx, and their external appearance, to the family of the *Tyrannidae*. However, in the covering of their feet these birds strikingly resemble the Singing Birds, in that they, at least on the outer posterior side of their feet, have a complete space, which extends to the edge of the dorsal side of the pes.

The most striking exceptions to this rule I find in the characters of the hinder plates; two hinder series of plates may appear (1) in Singing Birds with the muscular organ of voice (Larks); (2) in *Picarii* (*Gubernetes*); (3) in *Tracheophones* (*Thamnophilus, Chamaeza*,

---

[1] In the last systematic work, *The Genera of Birds*, by G. R. Gray, *illustrated with 350 plates*, this covering of the foot, which is so important in the classification of Genera and Families, is quite overlooked. Swainson had observed it.

Scytalopus). Further, from the characters of *Prionitis* (a bird without any laryngeal muscles), which possesses three series of hinder plates, we may see that the plates are the commencement of the granules.

In the third category of *Insessores*, the external characters are of no use to us in the *Tracheophones* with the tracheal organ of voice. There is among them *Myiothera*, a bird with the covering of its foot undivided at the sides. *Conopophaga* and *Tinactor* have indeed no tarsal scutes, but the anterior plates extend back to the inner side of the foot, and leave a space on the external hinder side only; other *Tracheophones* resemble the Larks in having two posterior series of plates, which meet on the hinder edge of the foot: *Thamnophilus, Chamaeza*, and *Scytalopus*. Other members of this family resemble the *Picarii* in the anterior plates, reaching, on each side, to a granulated space: *Anabates* and *Cinclodes*. In *Synallaxis* and *Dendrocolaptes* the anterior series of plates embraces the foot posteriorly, on its inner side, but on the external hinder side there lies a series of small scutes.

Certhia and *Tichodroma*, also, among the Singing Birds, have a series of plates on the hinder side externally, but the inner side is encased. There are consequently, among the Singing Birds, more forms of covering for the feet than the two described by Blasius and Keyserling.

The following practical rules may be deduced from this discussion, which may be useful in classifying birds not yet examined.

(1) There is no external character, from which, under all circumstances, it is possible to conclude with certainty what is the internal structure of the Passerinae, and chiefly, what is the structure of the organ of voice; and the characters of the covering of the feet are not, in single cases, to be relied on.

(2) The granulated or naked character of the dorsal surface of the foot is, so far as is yet known, a sign of the want of several separate anterior and posterior muscles in the muscular organ of voice; if, that is, the anterior plates extend, without break, from the lateral space to the granular posterior covering, or to the naked tract; whence we may conclude that *Pyroderus, Tijuca, Querula, Gymnoderus, Ptilogonys, Phytotoma, Lipaugus*, and *Agriornis* in the New World, and *Calyptomena* and *Promerops* in the Old World, although their larynges have not yet been examined, most probably do not possess the muscular organ of voice, with many muscles. *Promerops* clearly belongs to the *Upupinae*, the rest partly to the *Ampelidae*, partly to the *Tyrannidae*.

(3) Among the birds of the Old World no example is as yet known of the bilaminate tarsus existing without the muscular organ of voice; and consequently we may with great

safety place among the Singing Birds those East Indian and Australian forms, whose larynx has not yet been examined, but which are provided with the bilaminate tarsus; as *Epimachus, Pomatorhinus, Pitta, Myiophonus, Pachycephala, Fregilus, Grallina,* and *Paradisea.*

(4) For the birds of the New World the conclusion, from the presence of the tarsal scutes, that there exists a muscular organ of voice, does not hold. At any rate, there is something very much like the tarsal scutes, where the hinder side of the foot, both internally and externally, is devoid of either granules or plates; and the larynx with several muscles is absent.

(5) In those birds on the hinder side of whose foot are two series of large plates, no safe deduction as to the internal structure can be made, from their presence; indeed, this structure of the foot may be allied with the most various forms of internal structure.

(6) In South America this structure only appears in birds without the muscular organ of voice, and in particular, in several *Tracheophones.* The European form of Singing Birds with two series of plates behind, that is as in the Larks, does not appear at all in South America. What have been considered, in South America, as Larks, are partly species of *Furnarius,* and partly of *Centrites* (Cab.) The South American Passerines, therefore, with two series of large plates on the hinder side of the foot, which meet one another at its hinder edge, are to be placed by analogy with the already examined *Chamaeza, Thamnophilus,* and *Scytalopus,* along with the *Tracheophones,* even if we do not know the organ of voice, as in the cases of *Myiocincla* Sw., and *Pteroptochus* Kittl.

(7) Where the anterior plates of the foot pass right round to the hinder edge, it may be safely supposed that the larynx with many muscles is wanting, as in *Knipolegus* and *Entomophagus.* This never exists in company with the muscular organ of voice, but has always been observed when it is absent.

(8) Among the *Tracheophones,* whose larynx has been examined, there are genera allied to one another, of which one has the foot covered with two series of plates, and the other is without a horny covering on the external and internal parts of the hinder side, and is, as it were, encased. The latter can be recognised from their allies. This is the case, for example, with *Pithys* and *Grallaria,* which may very safely be supposed to be *Tracheophones. Chamaeza* bears the same relation to *Grallaria,* as *Thamnophilus* to *Myiothera.*

(9) Among the *Tracheophones* there is a form of covering for the foot, which in some genera cannot be accurately differentiated from that of the *Picarii,* and in others from that of the true Singing Birds.

In the following table I have put together those Passerines which want the larynx with many muscles, with their geographical distribution. With those whose larynx has been examined are also placed those for which we are able to conclude, from the above results, and rules, what their internal structure may be from their external characters. The names of the latter are printed in italics.

The *Scansores* are not added, in this table, as in the group of *Picarii* they hold together, and have pretty much the same form in the different divisions of the world.

Table of the Genera, without the Muscular Organ of Voice.

(The Genera printed in *italics* have not had their larynges examined, but are interpolated.)

	Old World.	New World.	Australia and Polynesia.
Thamnophilus Vieill.	.. ..	Thamnophilus	
Myiothera Ill.	.. ..	Myiothera	
Conopophaga Vieill.	.. ..	Conopophaga	
Pithys Vieill.	.. ..	*Pithys*	
Chamaeza Vig.	.. ..	Chamaeza	
Grallaria Vieill.	.. ..	*Grallaria*	
Furnarius Vieill.	.. ..	Furnarius	
Cinclodes Gray	.. ..	Cinclodes	
Tinactor Pr. M.	.. ..	Tinactor	
Anabates Temm.	.. ..	Anabates	
Anumbius Gray	.. ..	*Anumbius*	
Synallaxis Vieill.	.. ..	Synallaxis	
Dendrocolaptes Herm.	.. ..	Dendrocolaptes	
Dendroplex Sw.	.. ..	*Dendroplex*	
Glyphorhynchus Pr. M.	.. ..	*Glyphorhynchus*	
Dendrocincla Gray	.. ..	Dendrocincla	
Xiphorhynchus Sw.	.. ..	Xiphorhynchus	
Picolaptes Less.	.. ..	Picolaptes	
Sittasomus Sw.	.. ..	*Sittasomus*	
Dendrodromus Gould	.. ..	*Dendrodromus*	
Limnornis Gould	.. ..	*Limnornis*	
Enicornis Gray	.. ..	*Enicornis*	
Lochmias Sw.	.. ..	*Lochmias*	
Scytalopus Gould	.. ..	Scytalopus	
Pteroptochus Kittl.	.. ..	*Pteroptochus*	
Xenops Hoffm.	.. ..	Xenops	
Chasmarhynchus T.	.. ..	Chasmarhynchus	
Ampelis L.	.. ..	Ampelis	
Pyroderus Gray	.. ..	Pyroderus	
Gymnoderus Geoffr.	.. ..	Gymnoderus	
Cephalopterus Geoffr.	.. ..	Cephalopterus	

	Old World.	New World.	Australia and Polynesia.
Gymnocephalus Geoffr.	.. ..	Gymnocephalus	
Phytotoma Mol.	.. ..	Phytotoma	
Rupicola Briss.	.. ..	Rupicola	
Tijuca Less.	.. ..	Tijuca	
Phibalura Vieill.	.. ..	Phibalura	
Psaris Cuv.	.. ..	Psaris	
Pachyrhamphus Gray	.. ..	Pachyrhamphus	
Querula Vieill.	.. ..	Querula	
Eurylaimus Horsf.	Eurylaimus		
Corydon Less.	Corydon		
Cymbirhynchus Vig.	Cymbirhynchus		
Serilophus Sw.	Serilophus		
Psarisomus Sw.	Psarisomus		
Pipra L.	.. ..	.. Pipra	
Jodopleura Less.	.. ..	.. Jodopleura	
Calyptura Sw.	.. ..	.. Calyptura	
Calyptomena Raffl.	Calyptomena		
Tyrannus Briss.	.. ..	.. Tyrannus	
Scaphorhynchus Pr. M.	.. ..	.. Scaphorhynchus.	
Saurophagus Sw.	.. ..	.. Saurophagus	
Tyrannula Sw.	.. ..	.. Tyrannula	
Elaenia Sund.	.. ..	.. Elaenia	
Ptilogonys Sw.	.. ..	.. Ptilogonys	
Milvulus Sw.	.. ..	.. Milvulus	
Lipaugus Boie	.. ..	.. Lipaugus	
Myiobius Gray	.. ..	.. Myiobius	
Pyrocephalus Gould	.. ..	.. Pyrocephalus	
Setophaga Sw.	.. ..	.. Setophaga	
Arundinicola D'Orb. Lafr.	.. ..	.. Arundinicola	
Fluvicola Sw.	.. ..	.. Fluvicola	
Knipolegus Boie	.. ..	.. Knipolegus	
Taenioptera Bonap.	.. ..	.. Taenioptera	
Gubernetes Such.	.. ..	.. Gubernetes	
Agriornis Gould	.. ..	.. Agriornis	
Alecturus Vieill.	.. ..	.. Alecturus	
Lichenops Com.	.. ..	.. Lichenops	
Centrites Cab.	.. ..	.. Centrites	
Platyrhynchus Desm.	.. ..	.. Platyrhynchus	
Colopterus Cab.	.. ..	.. Colopterus	
Orchilus Cab.	.. ..	.. Orchilus	
Todirostrum Less.	.. ..	.. Todirostrum	
Todus L.	.. ..	.. Todus	
Trochilus L.	.. ..	.. Trochilus	
Phaëtornis Sw.	.. ..	.. Phaëtornis	
Orthorhynchus Cuv.	.. ..	.. Orthorhynchus	

General Remarks on the Classification of the Passerines. 45

	OLD WORLD.	NEW WORLD.	AUSTRALIA AND POLYNESIA.
Lampornis Sw.	.. ..	Lampornis	
Campylopterus Sw.	.. ..	Campylopterus	
Ornismyia Less.	.. ..	Ornismyia	
Merops L.	Merops	.. .. ..	Merops
Upupa L.	Upupa		
Promerops Briss.	Promerops		
Alcedo L.	Alcedo	Alcedo	Alcedo
Ceryle Boie	Ceryle	Ceryle	
Syma Less.	Syma	.. .. ..	Syma
Todirhamphus Less.	..	.. .. ..	Todirhamphus
Ceyx Less.	Ceyx	.. .. ..	Ceyx
Prionitis Ill.	.. .. ..	Prionitis	
Buceros L.	Buceros		
Coracias L.	Coracias		
Eurystomus Vieill.	Eurystomus		
Opisthocomus Hoffm.	.. ..	Opisthocomus	
Cypselus Ill.	Cypselus	Cypselus	Cypselus
Acanthylis Boie	.. ..	Acanthylis	
Caprimulgus L.	Caprimulgus	Caprimulgus	Caprimulgus
Antrostomus Gould	.. ..	Antrostomus	
Chordeiles Sw.	.. ..	Chordeiles	
Nyctibius Vieill.	.. ..	Nyctibius	
Podargus Cuv.	Podargus	.. .. ..	Podargus
Steatornis Humb.	.. .. ..	Steatornis	
Colius Briss.	Colius		
Musophaga Isert.	Musophaga		
Corythaix Ill.	Corythaix		
Chizaeris Wagl.	Chizaeris		

VI. GENERAL REMARKS ON THE CLASSIFICATION OF THE PASSERINES.

A superficial study of the birds examined with regard to the formation of their larynges, shews that the external forms of genera or families are repeated to a certain degree with varying larynges. There occur analogous external forms among Passerines with, and without, the vocal larynx. The forms analogous to the Swallows (*Hirundo*) with vocal larynx, among the birds without it are the Swifts (*Cypselus*); just in the same way the *Muscicapae* of the Old World (*Muscicapidae*) are related to the *Muscicapae* of the New (*Tyrannidae*), *Nectarinia* to *Trochilus*, the Ravens to the Rollers (*Coracias*), *Sylvia* to *Setophaga*, *Bombycilla* to *Ampelis*, the *Fringillidae* to *Colius*. Indeed one may sometimes find three forms of larynx in analogous birds. Those which Cuvier put under *Lanius* are an example of this:

    Lanius, Singing Bird.
    Thamnophilus, Tracheophone Bird.
    Psaris, Picarian larynx.

Or in Swainson's family *Lanidae:*

    Lanius, Singing Bird.
    Thamnophilus, Tracheophone Bird.
    Tyrannus, Picarian larynx.

A similar triad is formed by the three genera which Cuvier collected under *Muscicapa*, Swainson in his *Muscicapinae*, and Gray in his *Muscicapidae:*

    Muscicapa, Singing Bird.
    Conopophaga, Tracheophone Bird.
    Tyrannus, Picarian larynx.

So too the genera placed by Cuvier among the *Tenuirostres:*

    Certhia, Sitta, Nectarinia, Singing Birds.
    Furnarius, Xenops, Anabates, Synallaxis, Dendrocolaptes, Tracheophone Birds.
    Trochilus, Upupa, Picarian larynx.

Among the *Turdidae*, sub-family *Formicarinae* Gray, we again find the three forms of larynx, if it be supposed that *Dasycephala* agrees with the *Ampelidae* and *Tyrannidae*, in the structure of its larynx.

    Cinclus, Singing Bird.
    Myiothera, Tinactor, Chamaeza, Tracheophone.
    Dasycephala.

We can again find the triad among the *Troglodytinae* of Gray, who is willing to separate *Menura*, which has two laryngeal muscles on either side, from the Singing Birds:

    Troglodytes, Thrioturus, Singing Birds.
    Scytalopus, Tracheophone.
    Menura.

These comparisons are sufficient to show, at a glance, how unnatural and untenable are such combinations, since these birds are, by this means, completely removed from their natural allies, and are united by characters which are very unessential, such as the form of the beak, which passes by imperceptible gradations from *Lanius*, through *Icterus, Tanagra, Fringilla, Corvus, Sturnus, Turdus, Sylvia,* and *Certhia,* to the extreme forms. Those birds that have the hinder side of the foot covered with granules, which as a rule are also those with a simple larynx, are only united among themselves, and ought not to be mixed up with the Singing Birds who have tarsal scutes; in these comparisons *Ampelis*, *Psaris*, *Tyrannus*, *Dasycephala*, *Upupa*, and others, are separated from their true allies, and distributed among the quite different Singing Birds. The same holds for the Tracheophones, *Thamnophilus*, *Myiothera*, *Conopophaga*, *Chamaeza*, *Scytalopus*, *Furnarius*, *Anabates*, *Tinactor*, *Xenops*, *Synallaxis*, *Dendrocolaptes*, and others, whose forms of bill are in extreme cases, as *Thamnophilus* and *Dendrocolaptes*, very different, but pass into one another by imperceptible steps. Every one now sees that neither the Shrikes, nor the Fly-catchers, nor the Thrushes, nor the Wrens, nor the Tree-climbers are their allies, or the allies of any one of these genera; and that the *Tracheophones* must be brought together into one great family. Whoever has once examined the tongues of *Upupa*, *Buceros*, and *Alcedo* will see that these three genera belong together to one family (*Lipoglossi* Nitzsch), although their beaks have very different forms, and this is a further reason for thinking that a tribe of *Tenuirostres*, which brings together *Certhia*, *Furnarius*, *Dendrocolaptes*, and *Upupa*, would be just as artificial and unnatural as any of those families, which till the latest times, have been formed by systematists, without the assistance of anatomy.

Hence it may be concluded that every family of Passerines should only include birds with a similar larynx. We should not be able to bring together *Malaconotus* and *Thamnophilus*, *Bombycilla* and *Ampelis*, *Muscicapa* and *Tyrannus*, *Hirundo* and *Cypselus*, *Cinclus* and *Myiothera*, *Parus* and *Setophaga*, or *Corvus* and *Cephalopterus*, not to mention many other similar misconceptions, which are found in nearly every family of the systematist.

How far the orders of Passerines can be formed, according to the structure of their vocal organ, is another question. If we divide the Passerines, including the Scansores, according to the structure of their vocal organs, avoiding the errors introduced by Nitzsch, and by the aid of the knowledge lately obtained, into *Oscines* and *Picarii*, the two divisions would probably contain the following families:

I. *Oscines.*

Lanidae.	*Paradiseidae.*
Muscicapidae.	*Fringillidae.*
Turdidae.	*Tanagridae.*
Sturnidae.	*Sylvidae.*
Cinclidae.	*Hirundinidae.*
Meliphagidae.	*Alaudidae.*
Corvidae.	*Certhidae.*

II. *Picarii.*

Myiotheridae.		*Colidae.*
Scytalopidae.		*Prionitidae.*
Anabatidae {	*Anabatinae.*	*Meropidae.*
	Dendrocolaptinae.	*Lipoglossi.*
Ampelidae {	*Ampelinae.*	*Coraciadae.*
	Piprinae.	*Opisthocomidae*[1].
	Psarinae.	*Musophagidae.*
	Eurylaiminae.	*Galbulidae.*
Tyrannidae {	*Tyranninae.*	*Picidae.*
	Fluvicolinae.	*Cuculinidae.*
	Todinae.	*Bucconidae.*
Trochilidae.		*Trogonidae.*
Fissirostres {	*Cypselinae.*	*Rhamphastidae.*
	Caprimulginae.	*Psittacidae.*

I consider, however, the separation into *Oscines* and *Picarii*, as orders of birds of equal value with the other orders, and in the sense of Nitzsch, as untenable. It has already been shewn that external characters do not always allow us to speak with safety on internal structure, for there are many striking exceptions in the matter of the covering of the foot. Just as slight are the constant internal characters, which are found in company with various forms of larynx. The caeca are present in all Singing Birds that have the muscular organ of voice[2]. Passerines which have not the caeca are only found among those in which the muscular organ of voice is wanting, as *Cypselus*, *Alcedo*, *Buceros*, *Picus*, *Yunx*, *Rhamphastos*, *Psittacus*, *Chizaeris*, *Corythaix*, *Upupa*, and *Trochilus*. But the caeca are present in most of the Passerines which have not the muscular organ of voice, as, for example, *Chasmarhynchus*, *Ampelis*, *Rupicola*, *Psaris*, *Gymnocephalus*, nearly all the *Ampelidae* which I have examined, the *Tyrannidae* (also *Todirostrum*[3]),

---

[1] It is certain that *Opisthocomus* does not belong to the *Penelopidae*, from the fact that the penis discovered by Von Tschudi, which is formed in the *Penelopidae* (*Penelope, Crax*) on the type of that found in the three-toed *Ratitae* and in the Ducks, is completely wanting. The *Penelopidae*, but not *Crypturus* and *Hemipodius*, agree with the three-toed *Ratitae*.

[2] If Duvernoy (Cuvier, Leç. d'Anat, comp. 2nd ed.) did not find them in *Lanius, Gracula*, and *Paradisea*, it was, without doubt, through some mistake. Garnot mentions them in *Paradisea apoda*.

[3] According to Duvernoy they are wanting in *Todus*.

Thamnophilus, the Oven-birds, and their allies. The azygos carotid, from Nitzsch's own results, appears in so many of his *Picarii*, that I think it may be passed over; and I have already spoken of the complete valuelessness of the differences observed in the sternum.

But the separation of the larynx into two chief forms cannot be accurately carried out. The larynx of *Chasmarhynchus* has not its like in all the rest of the Passerines; it shares, at the same time, in the characteristics of the *Picarii* and the *Oscines;* according to its foot and habits it would belong to the *Ampelidae;* the muscles of its larynx act on the whole breadth of one ring, as in some *Tyrannidae*, and at the same time on the ends of a second ring, as in the Singing Birds; its muscular labium between the larynx and the first half-ring is altogether peculiar. The larynx of the Parrots with only a single glottis and three muscles, is just as peculiar. If the number of the anterior and posterior muscles of the Singing Birds is reduced in *Maenura*, there are also, even among the *Picarii*, examples of the single lateral muscle having an inclination to become divided into an anterior and a posterior portion, as in *Pipra leucocilla*, while it is undivided in the other *Piprae*. Among the *Tracheophones* the muscle of the larynx is sometimes single (*Thamnophilus*, *Myiothera*, and *Chamaeza*), sometimes double (*Furnarius*, *Synallaxis*, *Dendrocolaptes*, and others). If one can imagine the anterior and posterior muscles of *Maenura* to be broadened, we should get a single mass of muscle, as in *Chasmarhynchus;* and if, on the other hand, the muscles of *Chasmarhynchus* were divided in the middle, and the first ring had the same relations as the second, we should get the same muscular organ of voice as in the *Oscines*. Some of the *Picarii* differ from the general type, inasmuch as their muscle is no true lateral muscle, but acts on the ends of one ring; thus, the large muscle of *Trochilus*, which covers the anterior face of its larynx, only moves the posterior end of the second ring, and, from the posterior end of this ring there goes, in the opposite direction, a second small muscle, which I was the first to describe, to the succeeding rings, and which binds the half-rings together; of such a form no other example is found either in the *Oscines*, or in the *Picarii*. The muscular supply of the larynx in *Colius* is also peculiar, inasmuch as the lateral muscle of the larynx is divided into bundles for several half-rings; a condition which is quite unusual among the *Picarii*.

Finally, there are some Passerines which, notwithstanding the differences of their larynges, are remarkably like one another. I will not speak of the *Muscicapidae* of the Old and New World, which may be separated, as is already known, by the structure of their feet and wings, since it is only in the *Tyrannidae* that the foot is granulated, and the primaries perfect; but *Setophaga*, a Tyrannine, and *Sylvicola*, a Singing Bird, which resemble one another in the structure of the wing and of the foot, are strikingly alike, and are separated, according to Audubon, by the fact that *Setophaga* has the larynx of *Tyrannus*, and *Sylvicola* that of the Singing Birds. It must be said, and rightly, that one of the *Setophagae* is more allied to the Singing Birds than to the Parrots, whose larynx is very different to that of them both. From these remarks I do not conclude that *Setophaga* must be placed with the *Sylvidae*, but I contend that those divisions are unnatural which separate *Setophaga* and *Sylvicola*, and place them in perfectly different orders. The same holds for *Cypselus* and *Hirundo*. It is not right to place *Cypselus* and *Hirundo* in one family; but these Swallows are not so far separated from one another, that they can be placed in perfectly different orders.

It is, then, now thoroughly proved that the Singing Birds cannot be separated, as an order, from the rest of the Passerines. There is only one large division of *Insessores* or *Passerines* which must also include the *Scansores*. This order of *Insessores* includes birds with the most various supply of vocal muscles, as well as birds which do not possess these muscles. They pass imperceptibly into one another. In *Upupa* the lateral muscle of the trachea is inserted into the first, and slightly moveable, half-ring of the bronchus, and it is only a slight step from those in which it does no longer reach the bronchus, as in *Prionitis*, *Opisthocomus*, *Bucco*, *Trogon*, *Rhamphastos*, *Pteroglossus*, *Corythaix*, and *Chizaeris*. In these birds, however, there is not wanting that most general condition for the formation of voice—the possession of vibrating folds of membrane between the most moveable half-rings. Some have, also, further elements of it, as *Prionitis*, which has a very large *cartilago arytaenoidea* of the *membrana tympaniformis* attached to the lower larynx.

It is a further question, whether we can divide the *Insessores*, as an order, according to their larynges.

If the *Picarii* and *Oscines* are not orders of birds, they may perhaps be tribes of an order, and the same question may be asked about the *Tracheophones*. If these families may be divided into three sections, then we get the following series:

ORDO INSESSORES.

Tribus I. *Oscines s. Polymyodi.* Singing Birds.

Lanidae.	*Sturnidae.*
Muscicapidae.	*Meliphagidae.*
Turdidae.	*Cinclidae.*

Corvidae.	*Sylvidae*
Paradiseidae.	*Hirundinidae*
Tanagridae.	*Alaudidae*
Fringillidae.	*Certhidae.*

Tribus II. *Tracheophones.* Windpipe-voiced Birds.

Myiotheridae.   *Scytalopidae.*   *Anabatidae.*

Tribus III. *Picarii.* Pecking Birds.

Ampelidae.	*Opisthocomidae.*
Tyrannidae.	*Musophagidae.*
Trochilidae.	*Galbulidae.*
Fissirostres.	*Picidae.*
Colidae.	*Cuculidae.*
Prionitidae.	*Bucconidae.*
Meropidae.	*Trogonidae.*
Lipoglossi.	*Rhamphastidae.*
Coraciadae.	*Psittacidae.*

This classification is not free from objections, and it may be said against it, as would be said against the orders of *Oscines,* and *Picarii,* that *Setophaga* and *Sylvicola* are thus placed nearer to one another than *Setophaga* and *Psittacus*; and similarly *Hirundo* and *Cypselus,* nearer than *Cypselus* and the *Psittacidae.* If we further consider, that there are no external characters which correspond to internal structure, the most natural classification would be to simply make the families, carefully founded, and united by the form of their larynx, succeed one another in such a way that the Singing Birds and the Parrots should be at the ends.

Lanidae.	*Paradiseidae.*
Muscicapidae.	*Fringillidae.*
Turdidae.	*Tanagridae.*
Sturnidae.	*Sylvidae.*
Meliphagidae.	*Hirundinidae.*
Cinclidae.	*Alaudidae.*
Corvidae.	*Certhidae.*

Maenuridae.
Myiotheridae.
Scytalopidae.
Anabatidae.
Chasmarhynchidae.
Ampelidae.
Tyrannidae.
Trochilidae.
Fissirostres.
Colidae.
Prionitidae.
Meropidae.

Lipoglossi.
Coraciadae.
Opisthocomidae.
Musophagidae.
Galbulidae.
Picidae.
Cuculidae.
Bucconidae.
Trogonidae.
Rhamphastidae.
Psittacidae.

REMARKS.

The lists of the birds examined, which have been given, make it unnecessary to name separately those genera for which we have to wait, and the examination of which is desirable; they are principally Australian, Polynesian, and some East Indian genera also, specially from the Himalayas and the Sunda Islands.

What is now most wanted is a knowledge of the larynx of the Ant-birds of the Old World *Pitta* and its allies; the planta is undivided, as it appears to be in the Singing Birds only of the Old World, but the *Pittidae* are separated from the other Singing Birds by having ten complete primaries. According to a memoir by Herr Cabanis in the *Gesellschaft Naturforschender Freunde*, for August 18, 1846, Singing Birds have either only nine remiges on the manus, the first being completely wanting, or if present it is short. Since the *Maenuridae*, the larynx in which conforms to the type of the Singing Birds, are an exception to this rule; and since further the small size of the first primary in Singing Birds, if it is present, does not indicate any sharply marked distinction, inasmuch as in the Shrikes also the first feather is not unfrequently more or less diminished in size; it may be that in this external feature, just as in the investment of the foot, we must not expect any absolute character, which will hold for all cases, as affecting internal structure. In any case we must look with eagerness for the internal structure of *Pitta*. *Maenura* has two series of plates on the back of the tarsus, like the Larks and some *Tracheophones*.

I shall from time to time publish lists of lately examined genera of birds, and their larynges, so far as I shall be able to do so by the aid of fresh material. I hope the conviction that birds' skins without corresponding examples in spirits are now of little use, and that the latter are of greater value, will be made widely known among collectors.

DESCRIPTION OF THE FIGURES.

PLATE I. *CHASMARHYNCHUS.*

FIG. 1. Lower larynx of *Chasmarhynchus carunculatus*, seen from in front: natural size.

a. Trachea. *a'.* Lateral muscle of trachea. *b. Musculus sternotrachealis.* *c.* Laryngeal muscle. I. First, II. Second bronchial ring.

FIG. 2. The same from behind.

FIG. 3. The same from the side: magnified.

I. First bronchial ring, surrounded by muscle across its whole breadth. II. Second bronchial ring, the ends of which only are surrounded.

FIG. 4. The same from the side: natural size.

x. Nerve of the laryngeal muscle.

FIG. 5. Larynx of *C. carunculatus* from below; the tympanic membrane has been removed.

C. End of the muscle covering the anterior side of the larynx, which partly makes tense the tympanic membrane, and partly wraps itself round the end of the first and second half-rings. *c.* Transverse muscle lying on the anterior part of the pessulus, which makes tense the tympanic membrane.

FIG. 6. The same from below. The tympanic membrane is removed from one side, but is left on the other.

o. Pessulus. *o'.* Inner side of the outer boundary of the larynx. *c.* End of the muscle which covers the anterior side of the larynx, and surrounds the anterior end of the first bronchial ring, which is free from it on one side. *c'.* The portion of this musculature which surrounds the end of the second bronchial ring. *c²*. Transverse muscle on the anterior part of the pessulus, which serves to make tense the tympanic membrane. *c''.* Muscular fibres from the posterior portion of the larynx, which pass over the edge of the larynx to the tympanic membrane, and are partly continued into a muscular band *c'''*.

FIG. 7. Diagrammatic vertical section through the trachea and bronchi.

a. a. The last tracheal rings. *b.* The osseous larynx. *b'.* Pessulus. *c.* Muscles. *c².* The portion of muscular fibres, which pass between the lower end of the larynx, and the first bronchial ring, into the mucous membrane. *c³*. Mucous membrane. *d.* Labium of the glottis. *m.* Tympanic membrane. I. First bronchial ring.

Description of the Figures.

FIG. 8. Larynx of *Chasmarhynchus nudicollis*, seen from in front: of the natural size.

FIG. 8*. The same magnified.

a. Trachea. *a'*. Lateral muscles of the trachea. *b*. *Musculus sternotrachealis*. *c*. Muscles of the larynx. II. Second bronchial ring, the ends of which are covered by muscle.

FIG. 9. The same from below. The letters as before.

FIG. 10. The same from the side. The letters as before.

II. Second bronchial ring, the ends of which are covered by muscle, while the first is invisible, and is covered by muscle across its whole breadth.

FIG. 11. The lower edge of the bony larynx of *C. nudicollis*. *o*. Pessulus. *o'*. Outer and lower edge of the larynx. *o"*. Cartilaginous continuation of the larynx into the tympanic membrane.

FIG. 12. Lower face of the larynx of *Chasmarhynchus nudicollis*, with the first bronchial ring. The tympanic membrane has been removed.

I. First bronchial ring. *c*, *c'*. Muscle of the anterior portion of the larynx, which covers the end of the first (and second) bronchial ring. c^2. The portion of muscle, which covers the inner vocal cord *o*, and is continued forwards in the middle line of the pessulus. *c"*. Muscle of the hinder face of the larynx, which covers the cartilaginous projection (*o"* Fig. 11), and the ends of the first (and second) bronchial ring. *d*. *Labium externum*.

FIG. 13. Lower face of the larynx of *C. nudicollis*, and the commencement of the bronchi.

m. Tympanic membrane. *o*. Pessulus. II. Second bronchial ring. Letters as in Fig. 12.

FIG. 14. Diagrammatic section through the trachea and bronchi of *C. nudicollis*.

a. Trachea. *b*. Larynx. *b'*. Pessulus. *c*. Superficial layer of muscle, which is attached to the whole breadth of the first bronchial ring. c^2. The deeper layer, which is continued into the mucous membrane c^3, between the larynx and the first bronchial ring. *d*. *Labium externum glottidis*, outer vocal cord. *d'*. Inner vocal cord. *m*. Tympanic membrane.

PLATE II. *THAMNOPHILUS, MYIOTHERA, FURNARIUS*.

FIG. 1. Larynx of *Thamnophilus naevius*, × 7.

a. Membranous portion of the trachea. *b*. The fine half-rings in it. *c*. Lowest complete ring of the trachea. *d*. *Musculus sternotrachealis*. *d'*. The second head, where it is fastened to the lateral cord behind the laryngeal muscle, by the membranous portion of the trachea. *e*. Laryngeal muscle.

FIG. 2. Larynx of *Thamnophilus cristatus* Pr. M. The letters as before: × 6.

FIG. 3. Larynx of *T. guttatus* Spix. (*Lanius meleager* Licht.), × 8: the letters as before.

f. Lateral cord, which connects the fine half-rings of the trachea.

FIG. 4. Larynx of *T. cristatus* Pr. M., without the muscles. *f.* The lateral cord, which in this species is of cartilaginous consistency.

FIG. 5. Larynx of *Myiothera margaritacea* Mus. Berol. (*Turdus tintinnabulatus* L. Gm.) The same letters.

FIG. 6. Larynx of *Furnarius rufus*, × 8. From behind.

FIG. 7. From in front.

a. Membranous portion of the trachea. *b.* Its five rings. *f.* Bands which hold them together. *c.* Vocal ossicles placed on the first bronchial ring *c'*. *d.* Musculus sternotrachealis. *δ.* Lateral muscles of the trachea. *e.* Anterior and posterior laryngeal muscle. *o.* Cartilage in front of, and behind the trachea.

FIG. 8. Side view of the larynx of *Furnarius leucopus* Sw. Letters as before.

FIG. 9. The same with its muscles.

d. Musculus sternotrachealis. *e, e.* The two laryngeal muscles (the lateral muscle of the trachea is left out in this figure).

FIG. 10. Vocal ossicles and first bronchial ring, with the laryngeal muscles of the vocal ossicles of *Cinclodes*.

FIG. 11. The fine half-rings of the membranous portion of the trachea, in connection with its lateral band.

PLATE III. *TYRANNUS, ELAENIA, PLATYRHYNCHUS, ALCEDO.*

FIG. 1–5. Larynx of *Tyrannus sulphuratus*, × 4. Fig. 1, from in front. Fig. 2, 3, from the side. Fig. 4, from behind. Fig. 5, from below.

a. Lateral muscle of the trachea. *b.* Musculus sternotrachealis. *c.* Laryngeal muscle. 1. First bronchial ring. *x.* Cartilago arytaenoidea of the tympanic membrane.

FIG. 6–8. Larynx of *Tyrannus ferox* C. Fig. 6, from in front. Fig. 7, from the side. Fig. 8, from below. Letters as before.

d. Complete ring at the commencement of the bronchus.

FIG. 9, 10. Larynx of *Alcedo cabanisii* Tsch., seen from in front, and from the side. (The lateral muscle of the trachea is left out in the figure.)

FIG. 11–13. Larynx of *Elaenia pagana* Sund. Fig. 11, from in front. Fig. 12, from the side. Fig. 13, from below, × 5. Letters as in Fig. 1.

FIG. 14, 15. Larynx of *Platyrhynchus spec. peruana*. Fig. 14, from in front. Fig. 15, from the side. Letters as in Fig. 1, × 6.

FIG. 16–18. Larynx of *Elaenia brevirostris* Tsch., × 8. Fig. 16, from in front. Fig. 17, from the side. Fig. 18, from behind.

PLATE IV. *COLOPTERUS, PIPRA.*

FIG. 1–3. Larynx of *Colopterus cristatus* Cab.: magnified. Fig. 1, from in front. Fig. 2, from behind. Fig. 3, from the side.

a. Lateral muscle of the trachea.   *b.* Azygos muscle at the lower end of the trachea.   *c.* Muscle of the larynx.   *d.* Cleft at the hinder side of the lower part of the trachea filled up by a bony ridge, connected with the pessulus.

FIG. 4, 5.   Larynx of *Pipra auricapilla* Licht., × 4.   Fig. 4, from in front. Fig. 5, from below.

a. Last tracheal ring.   *a'.* Third bronchial ring.   *b.* Tracheal muscle.   *d.* Laryngeal muscle.

FIG. 6–8.   Larynx of *Pipra pareola*, × 6.   Fig. 6, 7, from in front.   Fig. 8, from behind.

a. Lateral muscle of the trachea.   *b. Musculus sternotrachealis.*   *c.* Laryngeal muscle. The hinder part of the lower part of the trachea is widely cleft, and in this space is placed a cartilaginous piece, which occupies also the lower ends of the first three bronchial rings, and takes the place of the pessulus.

FIG. 9–11.   Larynx of *Pipra leucocilla*, × 6.   Fig. 9, 10, from in front.   Fig. 11, from behind.

a. Lateral muscle as far as the third bronchial ring.   *b. Musculus sternotrachealis.*

PLATE V.   *TROCHILUS, ARUNDINICOLA, PYROCEPHALUS, MYIOBIUS, COLIUS.*

FIG. 1.   Larynx of *Trochilus dominicus*, × 5.   The muscles which covered one side of the larynx are removed.

a. Larynx.   *b.* First, very thin, *c.* Second, larger bronchial ring.   *d.* Laryngeal muscle as far as the hinder part of the second bronchial ring.   *e.* Second muscle, which arises from the hinder part of the second bronchial ring, and passes to the anterior face of the three succeeding bronchial rings.

FIG. 2.   The same larynx covered by the first muscle.

FIG. 3.   Larynx of *Trochilus dominicus*, from behind.

a. Larynx.   *c.* Hinder and triangular end of the second bronchial ring, into which is attached the large laryngeal muscle *d.*   *f. Cartilago arytaenoidea.*

FIG. 4.   Larynx of *Arundinicola leucocephala* D'Orb. Lafr. (*Todus leucocephalus* Pall.), × 8.

a. Lateral muscle of the trachea.   *b. Musculus sternotrachealis.*

FIG. 5.   The same from below, × 5.

x. Cartilago arytaenoidea.

FIG. 6.   Larynx of *Pyrocephalus coronatus* Gould (*Muscicapa coronata* L. Gm.), × 8.

a. Lateral muscle of the trachea.   *c.* Laryngeal muscle.

FIG. 7.   Larynx of *Pyrocephalus*, from below.

o. Pessulus.   *d.* Inner half-ring.   *e.* Outer half-ring.   *x. Cartilago arytaenoidea.*

FIG. 8.   Larynx of *Myiobius erythrurus* Cab. n. sp., × 8.

a. Lateral muscle of the trachea.   *b. M. sternotrachealis.*

Fig. 9, 10. Larynx of *Colius capensis*, from in front, ×4.

a. Musculus sternotrachealis. *b.* First large bronchial ring, with its scutiform prolongation. *c.* Laryngeal muscle to the scutiform prolongation of the first bronchial ring. *d.* Fasciculi of the same muscle for the three following half-rings.

Fig. 11, 12. The same larynx, from the side. The letters as before.

PLATE VI. *AMPELIS, RUPICOLA, GYMNOCEPHALUS, PSARIS, PACHYRHAMPHUS, CENTRITES, FLUVICOLA, DENDROCOLAPTES, CHAMAEZA, CONOPOPHAGA.*

Fig. 1, 2. Larynx of *Ampelis pompadora*, ×5.

a. Lateral muscle of the trachea. *b. M. sternotrachealis.*

Fig. 3. Larynx of *Rupicola cayana*, from the side, ×2.

a. Lateral muscle of the trachea. *b. M. sternotrachealis.*

Fig. 4. Larynx of *Gymnocephalus calvus* Geoffr.

a. Lateral muscle of the trachea. *b. M. sternotrachealis.*

Fig. 5. Larynx of *Psaris cayanus*, ×2; from in front. Letters as before.

Fig. 6. Larynx of *Pachyrhamphus atricapillus* Cab. (*Pipra atricapilla* Gm., *Lanius mitratus* Licht.), ×4; from in front.

a. Lateral muscle of the trachea. *b. M. sternotrachealis. c.* Laryngeal muscle to the second bronchial ring.

Fig. 7. Larynx of *Centrites rufus* Cab. (*Alauda rufa* aut.); from in front; magnified.

a. Lateral muscle of the trachea, covering it anteriorly. *c.* Laryngeal muscle.

Fig. 8. Larynx of *Fluvicola bicolor* (*Muscicapa bicolor* L. Gm., *M. albiventris* Spix.), from in front; magnified.

a. Lateral muscle of the trachea, covering it anteriorly. *c.* Laryngeal muscle.

Fig. 9. The same larynx from below.

a. Pessulus. *b.* Cartilago arytaenoidea. *c.* Tympanic membrane.

Fig. 10. Larynx of *Dendrocolaptes cayennensis*; from in front; magnified.

a. Membranous portion of the trachea. *b.* Fine tracheal rings in it. *c.* Vocal ossicles. *d. e.* The first two bronchial rings. *f.* Lateral muscle of the trachea. *g.* Anterior laryngeal muscle to the vocal ossicles. *h. Musculus sternotrachealis.*

Fig. 11. Larynx of *Chamaeza meruloides* Vig.; from in front : magnified.

a. Membranous portion of the trachea. *b.* Its fine rings. *c.* Vocal cartilage. *d. e.* The first two bronchial rings. *f.* Lateral muscle of the trachea. *h. M. sternotrachealis.*

Fig. 12. Larynx of *Conopophaga aurita* Vieill.; from in front: magnified.

a. Membranous portion of the trachea, with its five rings *b. c.* Lowest tracheal ring. *d. e.* The first two bronchial rings. *h. M. sternotrachealis. i.* Band.

PLATE VII.

Fig. 1. Syrinx of *Menura superba* from in front.
Fig. 2. The same from behind.
Fig. 3. The same laterally (right side).
Fig. 4. Syrinx of *Atrichia rufescens* from in front.
Fig. 5. The same from behind.
Fig. 6. The same laterally (right side).
Fig. 7. The syrinx of *Lipaugus cineraceus*. Left side.
Fig. 8. The same, front view.
Fig. 9. The syrinx of *Hadrostomus aglaiae*, front view.

PLATE VIII.

Fig. 1. Syrinx of *Grallaria guatemalensis*, posterior view.
Fig. 2. The same, anterior view.
Fig. 3. Processus vocalis of the same.
Fig. 4. Syrinx of *Hylactes megapodius*, front view.
Fig. 5. The same, back view.
Fig. 6. The syrinx of *Coracina scutata*, front view.
Fig. 7. The same, back view.
Fig. 8. The syrinx of *Pitta cyanura* from in front.
Fig. 9. The same from behind.
Fig. 10. The same laterally (right side).
Fig. 11. The syrinx of *Pitta angolensis*, front view.
Fig. 12. The same from behind.
Fig. 13. The same laterally (right side).

ADDENDUM TO MÜLLER'S PAPER ON THE VOCAL ORGANS OF PASSERINE BIRDS.

SINCE this paper has been printed fresh supplies of Singing Birds have been received from Jamaica, Venezuela, Guiana, and Mozambique. Of the American genera without the compound muscular organ; *Milvulus* Sw. (*M. tyrannus* Bonap.) and *Cyclorhynchus* Sundev. (*Platyrhynchus flaviventer* Spix.) have arrived for examination. The former genus is like *Tyrannus*, the latter has only one less-developed laryngeal muscle, which is little more than the mere continuation of the lateral muscle. *Todus viridis* L. has no muscle at all at the side of the larynx.

The examination of the genera *Setophaga* Sw. and *Myiadestes* Sw. was of especial interest. *Setophaga* had not been examined by me before, and there was only the observation of Audubon that *S. ruticilla* had merely a single laryngeal muscle, like the Tyrannidae. As such, I had therefore placed it in the list of birds without the complex vocal muscles, and had also supposed that this genus was closely allied to the singing genus *Sylvicola*. I am now convinced, by the examination of several examples of *Setophaga ruticilla*, that the results of Audubon are incorrect as regards this bird. Although its laryngeal muscles are comparatively feeble, yet they are distinctly arranged in an anterior and a posterior portion, so that *Setophaga* agrees, in the structure of its larynx, with *Sylvicola* and the Singing Birds in the true sense; this genus must be struck out from the list of birds without the complex vocal muscles, and be placed with the birds which have them. Their systematic position is not in the family of the *Tyrannidae*, but with the *Sylviadae*, and further close to *Sylvicola*.

Myiadestes Sw. is also a true Singing Bird, with the complex arrangement of singing muscles. I examined *M. genibarbis*, which is the type of the genus. This genus is very closely allied to *Ptilogonys* Sw. Gray formerly placed *Myiadestes* among his *Muscicapinae*, and *Ptilogonys* among his *Campephaginae* ('A List of the Genera of Birds'). In his later work ('The Genera of Birds') he has united both genera, and they are in fact very closely allied, if not identical. In any case it is now very probable that the type of the genus *Ptilogonys*, *Pt. cinereus* Sw., will also have the muscular organ of voice. Cabanis placed

Ptilogonys among the *Ampelidae*, in v. Tschudi's 'Fauna Peruana,' on account of the scutes on the lowest part of the pes; and for this reason I too placed *Ptilogonys* in the list of those Passerines, which probably lack the muscular organ of voice. After the examination of *Myiadestes genibarbis*, *Ptilogonys* must be struck out from it.

The following fresh genera with the muscular organ of voice have also been examined:

Buphaga Briss., *B. erythrorhyncha.*

Andropadus Sw., sp. affinis *A. importuno* Gray (*Trichophorus brachypodioides* Jard. Selb.), Mozamb.

Drymoica, spec. Mozamb.

Cyphorhinus Cab., *C. cantans* Cab., *Turdus Cantans* L. Gm.

Hylophilus Temm., *H. thoracicus* Temm.

Mniotilta Vieill., *M. varia* V.

Parula Bonap., *P. americana* (*Sylvicola americana* Audubon).

Spindalis Jard. Selb., *spec. Jamaic.*

Cardinalis Bonap., *spec. Columbiensis.*

Tiaris Sw., *T. lepida* (*Fringilla lepida* Gm.).

Sporophila Cab., *spec. Jamaic.*

APPENDIX.

THE unexpected nature of the facts brought forward in the preceding Memoir by its able author rendered it necessary that some changes should be made in the classification of the birds under consideration, or that the definitions of the families and orders should be modified accordingly. The researches of Nitzsch and his contemporaries had made it evident that the muscular organ of voice is present in all the Passeres up till their time examined. Its existence was therefore incorporated in the definition of the order. When Johannes Müller discovered that in many American genera previously included in the order—although their voice organs had not been examined—the vocal lower larynx is deficient, he assumed that the converse proposition was as true as that which states that all oscine birds are passerine. Subsequent ornithological investigation, however, has not substantiated the Müllerian dogma that all passerine birds are oscine, and the view which now receives almost universal acceptance is that the single order Passeres is composed of sub-orders and families, which, notwithstanding the differences in their larynges, are related among themselves too intimately for them to be separated by an ordinal difference.

The reasons for this view will now be considered seriatim. They rest upon the nature of—

I. *The foot.* In all Passeres the hallux is directed backwards, at the same time that digits ii, iii, and iv turn forwards. Among allied birds this is the case only in the Bucerotidae, Alcedinidae, Momotidae, Coliidae, Upupidae, Meropidae, Caprimulgidae, and Coraciidae.

II. *The pterylosis.* It is only in the Trogonidae that the pterylosis is the same as in the Passeres (vide Nitzsch's Pterylography).

III. *The colic caeca.* There are two short and narrow caeca coli, smaller than in any of the allied birds. Colic caeca are found also in the Trogonidae, Meropidae, Galbulidae, and Coraciidae.

IV. *The vomer.* The vomer is truncated in front, except in *Menura superba*, and runs forward as far as the line joining the anterior extremities of the separate maxillo-palatines. In the Capitonidae and Ramphastidae only among allied birds is the vomer truncated, but in them it ceases behind the maxillo-palatines, which sometimes fuse across the middle line, sometimes are free from one another.

V. *The sternum.* A single notch on each side (sometimes, as in *Heteralocha gouldi*, converted into a foramen) of the posterior margin of the sternum, divided into two in the Pteroptochidae, is found in all Passeres, at the same time that the manubrium sterni is large and bifid (but slightly so in *Chibia* and *Eurylaemus*).

VI. *The tensor patagii brevis muscle.* In the triangular patagium of the wing of the bird the tendons of two muscles are to be found. One is that of the *tensor patagii longus*, which forms the supporting cord of the free margin of the membrane itself. The second is that of the *tensor patagii brevis*, which courses parallel with the humerus, not distant from that bone, to the muscles and fasciae of the forearm. In the Ramphastinae, Capitoninae, and Picinae, where this muscle is less complicated than in any other birds, it arises, as is generally the case, from the apex of the upper of the two processes at the scapular extremity of the furcula, as well as by a small special slip from the superficial fibres of the *pectoralis major* muscle, which differentiates itself off from the main muscle near the upper part of its inserted extremity. The comparatively insignificant triangular or compound fleshy belly thus formed, with its apex directed towards the elbow, terminates in a cylindrical tendon, which, included between the layers of the fibro-cutaneous patagium, takes a straight course to its insertion into the axially-running tendon of origin of the *extensor metacarpi radialis longus* of Schöpss, at a short distance from the tubercle on the humerus whence the muscle springs.

As a result of this disposition, when the forearm is half-flexed, the tendon of the *tensor patagii brevis* is seen to enter the substance of the fibrous origin of the *extensor met. rad. longus*, and at right angles. This arrangement without any additions is characteristic of the Picariae, as defined by myself to include the three sub-families above referred to, and them only.

Among the Passeres a slight, but easily recognizable, difference in the manner of insertion of the muscle obtains. The similarly single cylindroid tendon runs from the muscular belly, which has its origin at the shoulder, as above described, to the upper margin of the *extensor met. rad. longus* muscle, at an exactly similar spot: it does not, however, simply blend with the fibrous origin of that muscle; it becomes attached to it at the spot indicated, and then (again considering the forearm as half bent upon the humerus) runs back *independently* to be attached to the base of the tubercle of origin of the *extensor met. rad. longus*, slightly below that muscle's springing-point. As a consequence of this arrangement there are two tendons to be seen running to one spot (that on the upper margin of the *extensor met. rad. longus*, where the tendon of the *tensor* meets it) from two points, one the apex of the tubercle on the humerus above referred to, and the other, the depression at its base. These tendons therefore converge as they leave the elbow, having at first an appreciable interval between them, which is gradually diminished as they approach, although they remain quite free from one another, that of the *tensor* being superficial.

I have had the opportunity of looking at this muscle in nearly 150 species of Passerine birds, belonging to nearly all the most important sections, including, among the more noteworthy genera—*Struthidea, Heteralocha, Diorurus, Prosthemadera, Melanocorypha, Strepera, Menura, Atrichia, Pitta, Rupicola, Lipaugus, Tyrannus, Chasmorhynchus, Pipra, Tityra, Hadrostomus, Cotinga, Furnarius, Picolaptes, Thamnophilus, Grallaria, Pteroptochus, Hylactes, Psarisomus* and *Serilophus*.

The only apparent exceptions I have found are the following. In *Pteroptochus albicollis* and in *Hylactes megapodius* the muscular fibres of the *extensor met. rad. longus* almost surround and enclose the tendons in question. Such being the case, the arrangement does not at first sight appear typically Passerine. Nevertheless, upon removing or pushing to one side these covering fibres, the two tendons are seen arranged exactly as in other members of the order.

In *Menura superba* and in *Atrichia rufescens*, feeble-winged birds again, the arrangement is not typical, and the disposition of the parts is almost exactly as in the Pici, as above described.

In other words there are not two tendons, one only being found, simple and broad, apparently produced by the blending of the two.

All other Passerine birds which I have examined follow the single type, differing only in the angular divergence of the tendons, their humeral attachments being much separated in most Sturnidae, Gymnorhinae, and Tyrannidae for example, but closely approximated in *Tropidorhynchus*, *Rupicola*, and others.

A short review of the peculiarities of the insertion of the *tensor patagii brevis* muscle in other birds will tend to render the importance of the character more clear, and may add some facts of interest in an ornithological point of view, for it is not in the least difficult for any one who has compared these structures in the various orders of the class to decide by an inspection of the outer surface of the elbow to which division any specimen belongs; and for the satisfaction of those naturalists who consider it essential that characters of importance should be verifiable on all occasions, it may be mentioned that from almost any skin it is possible to decide the point by soaking it, or the wing alone, in cold water, and carefully removing the tegument thus relaxed. On the present occasion the arrangement in the Anomalogonatae will also be almost solely discussed, although among the Homalogonatae characters of nearly equal significance are attainable, somewhat diminished in clearness in some cases by the diffused state of the tendons.

In the Galbulidae, as represented by *Galbula albirostris* and *Urogalba paradisea*, the tendon of the short *tensor* is simple, or it splits slightly before it meets the metacarpal extensor (where the distal moiety there terminates). Its main continuation sends back to the outer side of the lower end of the humerus a free fasciculus exactly like that above described in the Passeres, except that from about the middle of its lower margin a thin slip runs downwards and wristwards to the fascia of the ulnar side of the outer surface of the forearm.

In the Meropidae, as represented by *Merops apiaster* and *M. ornatus*, the only difference from the Galbulidae is that the distal branch is more clearly differentiated, and the slip to the ulnar side of the forearm is nearer the angular bend.

In the Coraciidae, as represented by *Coracias garrula* and a species of *Eurystomus* which was not in sufficiently good condition to be more definitely determined, there are two tendons parallel to one another, the anterior one of which runs to the superficial ulnar fascia before terminating, and sends wristwards a slip, like that in the Meropidae, to the long *extensor*. There is a passeriform free tendon running back to the lower end of the humerus from the outer tendon.

In the Trogonidae, as exemplified by *Trogon mexicana*, *T. puella*, and *Pharomacrus mocinno*, the condition is very complicated. A superficial long muscular mass runs nearly to the long extensor of the forearm. It has a short broad tendinous insertion into the fascia of the outer surface of the forearm; and this is specially developed in a line running back to the humerus in a passeriform manner. Deep of this are two parallel tendous: the one nearer the humerus terminates exactly like the single one of the Passeres; that further off ends as in the Pici above described.

In the Caprimulgidae, as found in *Caprimulgus europaeus* and *Chordeiles texensis*, the arrangement is almost exactly the same as in the Meropidae. The second outer tendon, however, is shorter.

K

In the Macrochires, including the Trochilidae and the Cypselidae, as found in many genera and species, the arrangement is uniform. The fleshy belly runs on to a special tendon which springs from the lower end of the outer surface of the humerus (where the horizontal slip in the Passeres terminates), and is continued, parallel to the forearm, along the radial margin to the hand. The tendon of the *tensor patagii brevis* is not developed, being replaced by the fleshy continuation of the muscle.

In *Upupa epops* the arrangement is fairly simple. The main tendon runs past the free lateral margin of the long *extensor* to the ulnar superficial fascia, where it becomes lost. It sends forward a fasciculus from about its middle, to end like the similar band in the Meropidae. Its difference from the passerine arrangement is well marked.

In the Bucerotidae, as found in several species of *Buceros*, *Toccus*, and *Bucorvus*, the only difference from *Upupa* is that the extra outer fasciculus is very much shorter. The lengthy tendon from the major pectoral is particularly large.

In the Alcedinidae the differences are so considerable and peculiar in the several genera that the muscle in this order has not been fully worked out as yet.

In the Momotidae the condition is the same as in the Coraciidae, except that the outer tendon does not split, and therefore sends forward no wristward slip. This condition I have found in *Momotus lessoni*, in *M. aequatorialis*, in *Eumomota superciliaris*, and in *Todus viridis*. The extension onwards to the ulnar superficial fascia springs from the portion of the horizontal tendon intermediate between the points of junction of the two parallel long tendons, and is not a direct continuation of either. It is frequently very thin.

As the Cuculidae and Musophagidae are frequently included together with the families above referred to, the arrangement of the short tensor in those birds must be mentioned. In all the Cuculidae the undivided tendon runs on to the ulnar superficial fascia without any complication. In the Musophagidae the whole tendon is comparatively feeble, and, if it were more definite at its margins, would be exactly like that in *Upupa*.

Next, with reference to the division of the order Passeres into minor sections.

In 1831 the late Professor C. J. Sundevall discovered the important fact that is expressed in the 1872 edition of his valuable 'Methodi naturalis Avium disponendarum Tentamen' in the following words :—' Hallux ..... per se mobilis. Musculus enim *flexor hallucis longus* articulum ejus ultimum flectens, a flexore digitorum communi perfecte solutus. (In avibus reliquis omnibus tendo hujus musculi cum tendinibus alterius conjungitur. Hallux igitur simul cum reliquis digitis semper flectitur.)' *Upupa epops*, agreeing with the Passeres in this respect, is by the author included with them. Recently, however, I have found reason for overthrowing the character, because in the Eurylaemidae there is a strong vinculum which joins the two muscles exactly in the same manner as in many of the non-passerine families.

Eurylaemus ochromelas, *Cymbirhynchus macrorhynchus*, and *Calyptomena viridis* are the species which I have examined (more than one specimen of each); and in all of them there is a narrow but strong vinculum, situated just above the metatarso-phalangeal articulations, and running from the tendon of the *flexor hallucis longus* downwards to the tendon of the *flexor digitorum profundus*. No other passerine bird which I have dissected possesses this vinculum.

not even *Rupicola crocea*, which has been thought by some to be intimately related to the Eurylaeminae.

Such being the case, I cannot do otherwise than divide the Passeres into two main sections—the Eurylaeminae, and the rest, because in all other essential respects they agree.

Four or five pairs of muscles running to the ends of the topmost three bronchial semi-rings constitute the Oscine syrinx, the distinctive features of which are therefore its Acromyodian and complex nature. MM. Keyserling and Blasius were the first to associate with this the bilaminate planta—an exception to which occurs in the case of the Alaudidae, as we all know, these birds possessing a divided planta together with an Oscine syrinx. In *Heteroonemis naevia*, as has been shown by Mr. Strickland[1], the planta is indistinguishable from that of the bilaminate Oscines. With reference to this and closely allied genera it must be noted that the scutellation of the front of the tarsus is also obliterated, so that the simplicity of the planta is only a participation in the condition which obtains in the tarsus generally. Therefore, with this exception (which from its associations can hardly be looked upon as such), it may be said as yet that *no bird which is not acromyodian has a bilaminate planta*.

Nevertheless the law enunciated by Cabanis, to the effect that when in a Passerine bird possessing ten primary remiges the first is long, then that bird is not Oscine (or Acromyodian), but 'Clamatorial' (or Mesomyodian), led that able ornithologist to place *Pitta* in the latter group, although it possesses a bilaminate planta; since which time Johannes Müller is not the only biologist who has wished to know the nature of the syrinx of that bird, of which Sundevall[2], in 1872, remarks, 'musculi laryngis inferioris ignoti.'

In *Pitta angolensis* the unmodified trachea terminates thoracically in a ring, split behind, and deep in front; which, from the fact that it presents irregularly placed fenestrae on its anterior surface, arranged in a somewhat transversely linear manner, appears to have been formed by the fusion of two rings. This terminal segment of the trachea does not, as in the Oscines and several other Passeres, form a three-way piece, because there is no antero-posterior bar traversing its inferior margin in the middle line. Of this, however, there is an indication in the form of a median backward-directed process, which advances a short distance into the inferior membraniform completion of the tube, from its anterior border. The tracheal ring last but one is complete, and has a slight median indentation in its inferior margin behind. These points are seen in Plate VIII, figs. 11–13.

The first and second bronchial ring-segments are semi-rings—not modified into the somewhat separate, round-margined, slightly oblique semicircles of fibro-cartilage or bone which, as usual, are found nearer the lungs—but are like moieties of true tracheal rings, approximate, sharp-edged, and at right angles to the axis of the tube. They present no peculiar processes, and are slightly swollen at their anterior extremities.

There is only a single pair of bronchial muscles, continued down from the sides of the

---

[1] Annals and Mag. Nat. Hist. 1844, vol. xiii, p. 415.
[2] Method. nat. Av. disp. Tentamen, 1872, p. 5.

windpipe; insignificant in size; quite lateral, and terminating by being inserted into the middle of the outer surface of the second bronchial semi-ring of each side.

Pitta cyanura differs from *P. angolensis* only in detail, not in plan of conformation. There are four instead of two syringeal bronchial semi-rings, to the middle of the last of which the single extremely feeble lateral muscle is attached on each side. In it also the last two tracheal rings, and not the last only, are incomplete behind, the last presenting a greater gap than the one above it. This syrinx is figured in Plate VIII, figs. 8–10.

Pitta is therefore mesomyodian, in which respect it differs from all the known Old-World Passeres except the Eurylaemidae—although *Philepitta*, with its lengthy first primary, is most probably the same in this respect.

The syrinx of *Coracina scutata* has been described by Professor H. Burmeister[1], and in Plate VIII, figs. 6 and 7, his figures are reproduced. The organ is mesomyodian and different from that of any known bird, more resembling that of *Gymnocephalus calvus* than any other. The lowermost tracheal ring blends in the middle line behind with the one next above it, whilst in front it sends down a median process to the topmost bronchial rings which fuse at the point of junction, although they are independent of one another posteriorly. The second bronchial semi-rings are strong, as are the topmost; broad at their outer margins and directed downwards at their anterior ends to meet a peculiar process which is directed upwards from the upper edge of the middle of the anterior surface of each of the third bronchial semi-rings. The fourth and the fifth bronchial semi-rings are stronger than is usually the case, and the true normal bronchus begins below them. There is a single pair of narrow lateral muscles which are inserted into the middles of the fifth bronchial semi-rings.

Among Tracheophone and other Mesomyodian Passeres the syrinx in the following genera and species has been described by myself alone.

Hylactes megapodius.—In this species the syrinx is not identical with any of those described by J. Müller. It does not differ much from those of *Scytalopus indigoticus* and *Chamaeza brevicauda* in its essential structure. By Müller, however, no mention is made of a peculiarity which I find in this species, which seems to me to throw some light upon the method of development of the tracheophone syrinx. This consists in the way in which the characteristic very slender rings of the specialised voice-organ, instead of ceasing abruptly at its upper end, continue upwards on the anterior surface of the trachea for a considerable distance, whilst posteriorly they suddenly change their breadth superiorly where the syrinx ceases. Figures 4 and 5, Plate VIII, represent the anterior and posterior views of the organ.

The *processus vocales*, which rest on the first and second modified and ossified bronchial semi-rings, extend up as far as the tracheal true ring, twelfth from the bottom. These twelve lowermost tracheal rings are incomplete opposite the *processus vocales* (in other words, at their sides), as they are in all the Tracheophonae; and the lowest is also broken, as it were, in the middle line behind.

Posteriorly the lower nine are extremely slender; the tenth (counting upwards) is somewhat

---

[1] Abhandlung der Naturforschenden Gesellschaft zu Halle, 1856, p. 205.

thicker, the eleventh still more evidently so, whilst the twelfth is as thick as any of the superior rings.

Anteriorly there are twenty-three of the lower tracheal rings, which are quite slender in the middle line, especially the three lowest; and of these the twelve lowest (those split laterally) are slender from one side to the other, whilst the upper eleven appear thick at their extreme ends on account of the intrusion, for a short distance round the sides of the tracheal tube, of the thickening above recorded of their hinder parts, which diminishes rapidly in a spindle-pointed manner.

The lowest tracheal ring is as slender as those just above it; and it is worthy of note that the *processus vocales* rest upon the thickened second bronchial semi-ring as well as on the first. These vocal processes cannot be detached from the sides of the trachea without injuring it; and the sterno-tracheal muscles arise from their apices, to which are also attached thin muscular sheets which extend up the windpipe laterally and a little posteriorly.

Grallaria guatemalensis.—In this species also the specialised syrinx does not cease abruptly at its upper end, the superior rings of the trachea, which help to constitute it, gradually losing their individual character. Figs. 2 and 1, Plate VIII, represent the front and back view of the organ, which is peculiarly shallow for its width, and involves but six of the lowermost tracheal rings. These six are incomplete at their sides where they are in contact with the *processus vocales*, which latter are small, flat, fusiform ossifications, pointed both at their upper and lower ends, and just touch the upper of the two superior enlarged and ossified bronchial semi-rings, the remainder of each bronchus being of the normal character. The last tracheal ring is incomplete in the middle line in front, as well as at the sides, whilst behind it is thickened, and sends small downward processes on each side of the middle line in such a manner as to develop a notch between them. Figure 3 represents the left-side view of these structures, seen from the interior of the organ, as well as the *processus vocalis*. From figure 2 it can be seen that the tracheal rings four, five, and six from the bottom are not ossified at all in front, and that rings seven, eight, and nine are only so at their sides, whilst ring ten, with those just above it, are extremely thin in the middle. Posteriorly also, from figure 1 it can be inferred that the rings above the lowest ones are very slender, becoming thicker by degrees above the sixth, which is the highest of those constituting the voice-organ.

With reference to the muscles, it may be stated that the lateral muscle of the trachea on each side covers and joins the upper extremity of the *processus vocalis*, turning off to become the *musculus sterno-trachealis* opposite the ring third from the end, and sending no continuation on to act directly upon the bronchial semi-rings.

Lipaugus cineraceus.—In this species the single specimen at my disposal has the lower part of the windpipe considerably damaged by shot. Nevertheless, as one side is comparatively uninjured, I have been able to make out the essential points in the structure of the syrinx, which does not differ much from that of *Pipra leucocilla*, as represented by Müller. The lowermost rings of the trachea are not peculiar, each one being deep, and meeting, at its superior and inferior margins, the rings above and below it. The first and second bronchial semi-rings resemble those of the trachea in their flatness, depth, and approximation, the third being the first normal bronchial ring. It, with those which follow, are slightly peculiar in that they are ossified throughout, except in a small part, equal to about one sixth the breadth of each semi-ring, one third distant from their anterior ends, where they retain their primitive cartilaginous structure (*vide* Plate VII, figs. 7 and 8).

The lateral muscle of the trachea is of considerable breadth, being most developed anteriorly, those of the opposite sides coming nearly into contact in the middle line in front. Opposite the tracheal ring seventh from the bottom, the small sterno-trachealis is differentiated off from the posterior portion of this muscle, by far its larger anterior part continuing downwards to become the intrinsic muscle of the syrinx, which ceases at its insertion into the anterior half of the third bronchial semi-ring. It exhibits no tendency to split into two as in *Pipra leucocilla*.

It may be mentioned that the second bronchial semi-ring is somewhat expanded at its ends, intruding more into the membranous completion of the bronchial tube than do those which follow it. The damaged condition of my specimen makes it impossible to determine whether the antero-posterior bar, which is situated at the point of bifurcation of the trachea, is formed by the last tracheal ring, or by the completion and junction of the first bronchial rings of either side. I am inclined to think it depends on the latter of these conditions. *Chiromachaeris manacus*, according to the description given by Müller, agrees exactly with this species, as far as its syrinx is concerned.

Heteropelma verae-pacis is most simple in its voice-organ. The single broad lateral muscle of each side of the trachea continues down to the middle of the second bronchial semi-rings, which is scarcely different from those below it either in bulk or appearance; and the one above it resembles it. There is, however, a considerable interval between it and the third, whilst it almost touches the first. None of the lowermost tracheal rings are peculiar in any way.

Hadrostomus aglaiae is a bird in which the calibre of the lower end of the trachea is very inconsiderable, and the syrinx is correspondingly difficult to investigate. The tracheal rings are not modified, except the last, which is developed into a three-way piece from the presence of a bar running from before backwards at the middle of the lower margin. The first bronchial half-ring is of the same flattened and deep nature as the tracheal rings, and, like them also, is not separated from the three-way piece by any interval. To its anterior end, on each side, as well as to the front of the three-way piece, the intrinsic muscle is attached, which descends, broad and thin, down the front of the lower part of the trachea, in contact with its fellow of the opposite side, there to terminate (*vide* Plate VII, fig. 9).

The second bronchial semi-ring is not modified. It is separated by a short interval from the first, and by a strikingly considerable one from the third, which is the commencement of the normal bronchus. I could not find that the muscles of the syrinx sent any fibres to this second ring, as in *Pachyrhamphus *atricapillus*, described by Müller, although otherwise this structure is almost identical in the two birds. If they are present they must be extremely feeble; and the relative distances of the upper bronchial semi-rings favours the view that some special arrangement exists.

The account, above given, of the voice-organs in the aberrant Passeres in question, is entirely confirmatory of the results arrived at by Johannes Müller. Both *Hylactes* and *Grallaria* are completely tracheophone, as he predicted they would be found to be, although they agree with one another, and differ from those previously described in having the syringeal end of the trachea less abruptly distinguishable as being composed of two parts. Neither *Lipaugus*, nor *Heteropelma*, nor *Hadrostomus* are far from the Mesomyodian types already known, as far as their voice-organs are concerned, which structural agreement clearly shows that our nomenclature is an inefficient one when it places *Hadrostomus* as far from *Pachyrhamphus* as either is from *Tityra*.

Again, also, that the Pipridae and Cotingidae should be considered to be different families is not borne out by the nature of the lower larynx; and it seems hardly possible to allow a difference in tarsal scutellation to constitute a family difference, when not borne out by more important points of internal structure.

Menura superba is another bird in which our knowledge of the structure of the syrinx is very deficient. Mr. Eyton has described it[1]; but his account will bear supplementing. He tells us that 'in addition to the usual sterno-tracheal muscles this curious bird has two other pair, both of which have their origin on the rings of the trachea on each side, at the point where it enters the cavity of the thorax. The anterior pair is inserted on the knobs at the extremities of the fourth bones of the bronchiae; the posterior pair are also inserted on the bronchiae, but on the three uppermost rings and on the posterior extremity of the fifth.'

In *Menura superba* the last sixteen rings of the trachea are peculiarly narrow from above downwards. These are carinate in front; in other words, instead of being flattened from without inwards (as is usually the case, and is so in the rings above the sixteenth in this bird), they are compressed from above downwards, by which means a sharp-edged ridge is developed, which projects outwards a short way beyond the level of the interannular membrane. The lowest of these rings, the last tracheal, whilst participating in this peculiarity, is modified to form the three-way piece, whence start the bronchi, an antero-posterior bar joining the downward-directed angles which are developed on the middle of the front and back of the ring, and supporting the syringeal semilunar membrane.

As in the typical Oscines, the first three bronchial semi-rings participate in the formation of the syrinx, and are modified accordingly, being stronger, deeper, more flattened, and more approximate than those which follow. The first of these is simple; the second is peculiar in being hollow and thin-walled, broader in front than behind, and broadest a short distance (about equal to its depth at the spot) posterior to its anterior extremity; the third is narrower, and terminates behind by a short descending hook.

The syringeal muscles are three in number on each side at their insertion, although at their origin only two can be distinguished. These are an anterior and posterior longitudinal, which, from a lateral point situated opposite the tracheal ring 19 above the last one, diverge forwards and backwards to the tips of the bronchial semi-rings. In Plate VII, figs. 1, 2, and 3, the front, back, and side views of the syrinx of *Menura* are figured.

The *anterior longitudinal* muscle, whose diameter is about four times that of the *depressor tracheae*, is of uniform size throughout, being constituted of parallel fibres. It is inserted into the lower margin of the expansion at the anterior extremity of the second bronchial semi-ring, at a short distance behind its apex.

The *posterior longitudinal* muscle, from being single above, divides into two below.

---

[1] Ann. & Mag. Nat. Hist. 1841, vol. vii, p. 49.

Before proceeding further it will be necessary to explain the way in which these muscles arise. There is a large air-cell, the anterior thoracic[1], in which the syrinx and base of the heart are situated. The visceral walls of this cell are so thin that the trachea may, to all intents and purposes, be said to perforate it. Where it does so, the membrane blends with its fascial sheath most intimately; and it is from the thus formed ring of junction that the long fibres of the syringeal muscles spring. This ring is not a simple horizontal circle of fibrous tissue surrounding the trachea. In its anterior half it is so; but behind it descends for some distance on each side to a median spot situated below its general level, at a distance beneath it equal to the diameter of the tube itself, to blend at the angle thus formed with a strong fibro-cartilaginous ribbon, which expands below the level of the tracheal bifurcation, to terminate as a membranous covering to the front of the oesophagus.

From the postero-lateral portion of the horizontal moiety of the ring just described, and from its descending limb the posterior longitudinal muscle of the syrinx arises on each side, powerful, and in a single mass, of which the longer postero-external fibres, as it descends, differentiate themselves off to form an independent fasciculus, which is inserted into the posterior hooked extremity of the third bronchial semi-ring. The other much larger internal portion, composed mostly of shorter and more oblique fibres, is inserted into the posterior triangular surface of the tracheal three-way piece (last tracheal ring), and into the posterior extremity of the first bronchial semi-ring, a few of its tendinous fibres of termination apparently running on to the back of the membrane between the first and second semi-ring, and perhaps slightly to the back of the second semi-ring itself, although this last seems to be independent in this respect.

The comparatively slender *musculus sterno-trachealis* springs from the lateral surfaces of the four or five tracheal rings above the last two, emerging between the anterior and posterior intrinsic muscles.

Menura superba, from the above description, is therefore Acromyodian, although not typically Oscine.

Atrichia rufescens presents very much the same arrangement as *Menura*. There are three modified bronchial semi-rings, the third descending posteriorly, and the second expanded a short distance before it reaches its anterior termination, the anterior longitudinal muscle being there inserted. The posterior muscle, however, does not clearly separate into two before it reaches its points of insertion, which are identical with those in *Menura*. The lower tracheal rings are different, in that they are not flattened from above downwards; they retain the characters of those above them to a great extent. The last forms the characteristic three-way piece. In Plate VII, figs. 4, 5, and 6, these points are clearly seen.

Atrichia is therefore also acromyodian, although far from being normally Oscine. It would require but little modification in either it or *Menura* to convert their syringeal muscular masses into more numerous independent muscles. In the Crow, Starling, and most of the other Oscines I have examined, the third semi-ring is the one to which the long anterior muscle runs, the long posterior not going beyond the second. This condition is just reversed

---

[1] *Vide* Owen's 'Anatomy of Vertebrates,' vol. ii, p. 211.

in the two birds under consideration. In the Finches the arrangement described by Cuvier obtains, both anterior and posterior long muscles running to the third bronchial semi-ring.

There is another feature in Passerine anatomy which has interested me considerably during my investigations. It is the rule among birds, almost without exception, that the main artery of the leg is that which must be supposed to be represented in Man by the *comes nervi ischiatici*, it accompanying the sciatic nerve—the sciatic artery. The main nerve of the leg is the sciatic; the main vein the femoral. The only known exceptions to this rule are the cases of the genus *Dacelo* among the Alcedinidae, and *Centropus* among the Cuculidae. In the former the femoral vein is replaced by the one which is intermediate in situation between its usual course and the sciatic artery; in the latter the sciatic artery is absent, and is replaced by the femoral[1].

In a certain few Passerine birds the main artery of the leg is the femoral, and not the sciatic. These genera are all members of the Oligomyodi of Müller; and the accompanying list contains the names of all the Oligomyodian species which I have had the opportunity of examining, with the results arrived at, as far as this peculiarity is concerned.

Passeres Oligomyodi.

With a femoral artery.	With a sciatic artery.
Chiroxiphia linearis,	*Mionectes oleagineus*,
Chiromachaeris vitellina,	*Tyrannisous vilissimus*,
Heteropelma veraepacis,	*Pitangus sulphuratus*,
Tityra personata,	*Myiodynastes luteiventris*,
Hadrostomus aglaias,	*Empidonax minimus*,
Lipaugus cineraceus,	*Myiarchus crinitus*,
Cotinga cincta,	*Tyrannus melancholicus*,
Chasmorhynchus nudicollis.	*Rupicola crocea*,
	Pitta angolensis,
	Pitta cyanura.

I must mention also that in a specimen of the minute *Mitrephorus phaeocercus*, it appeared to me that the artery of the leg was the femoral; but I should like to see more specimens before I can feel justified in disturbing any generalisations by using this single example.

All Acromyodian Passeres of species which I have examined, over one hundred in number, possess the sciatic artery, including *Menura* and *Atrichia;* and the Tracheophonae quite agree with them in this respect. Such being the case, it seems to me that from among the Mesomyodian Passeres a small section may be divided off, including the families Pipridae and Cotingidae, in which a characterising feature is the development of a femoral in place of a sciatic artery; and this being the case, *Rupicola* must be removed from the Cotingidae.

Although our knowledge of the classification of the Passerine Birds is still so far from complete, a digest of the facts at our disposal, based upon those brought forward in the work

---

[1] Proc. Zool. Soc. 1873, p. 629.

to the translation of which these latter pages form an appendix, together with the observations of later authors, makes it evident that of the whole Order the *Eurylaemidae* are the least specialized, so that they can hardly form other than a main division by themselves. Of the remainder *Pitta, Rupicola*, the Tyrannidae, the Tracheophonae together with the Pipridae and Cotingidae constitute a section for which I have suggested the name Mesomyodae in contrast to the Acromyodae (or Oscines), in which latter the syringeal muscles are inserted into the extremities of the bronchial semi-rings.

There is every reason for hope that by continued investigation into the osteology of the Passeres, so ably commenced by Professor Parker, and into the structure of their soft parts, the acute discrimination evinced by those who study skins alone in the determination of generic relations will be supplemented by an amount of information with reference to the affinities of the families which will before long lead to a correct estimate of the true classification of the order.

In conclusion it must be mentioned that this appendix is an incorporation of matter published in the Proceedings of the Zoological Society of London between the years 1873 and the present time; and that those new facts which its author has been able to bring forward are based upon specimens which he has had the opportunity of examining in his capacity of Prosector to the Zoological Society, as well as upon an extensive series of birds in spirit, most kindly placed at his disposal by Mr. Osbert Salvin. To Mr. P. L. Sclater the editor is also greatly indebted for information and advice on many points connected with the above investigation as well as for his kindness in revising the proofs of this work.

A. H. GARROD.

June 18th, 1878.

Zu Herrn Müller's Abhandlung über die Stimmorgane. Jahrgang 1845. Tab. I.

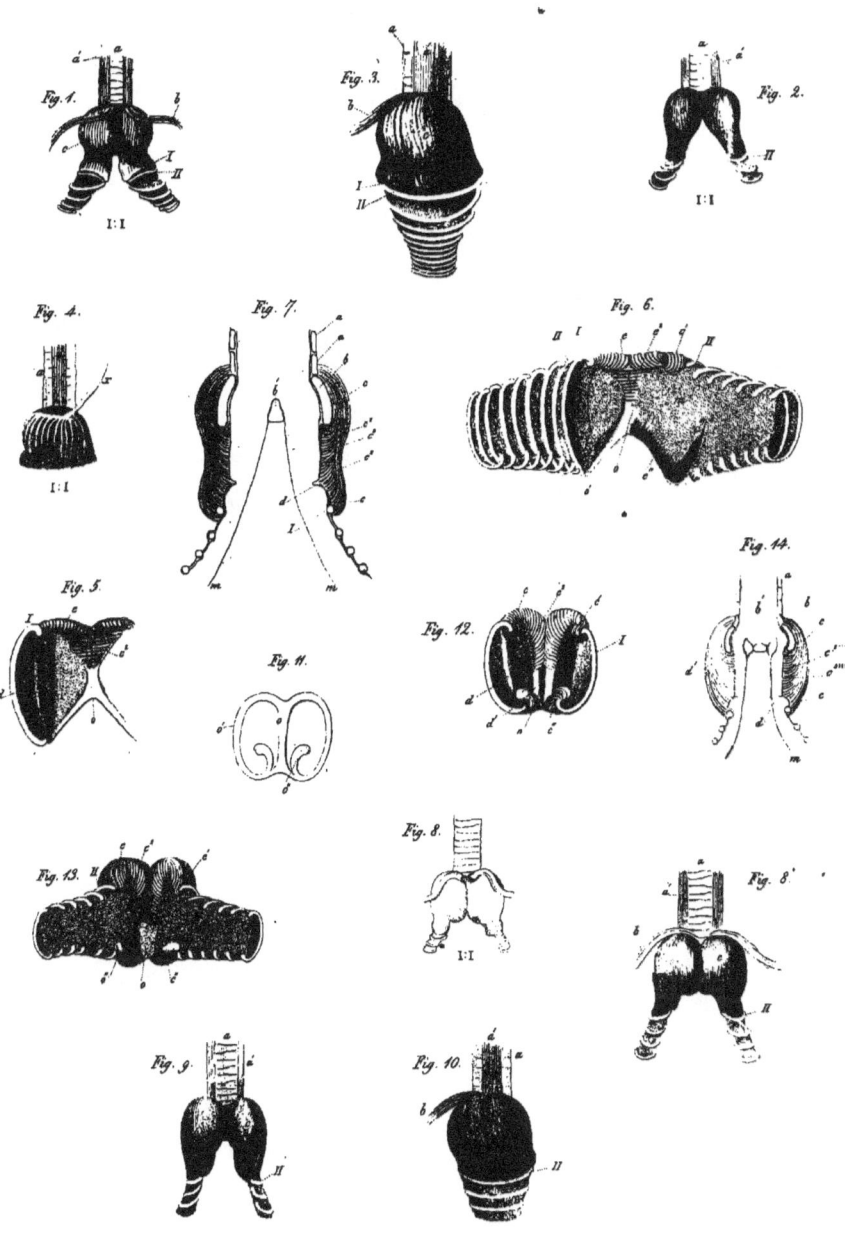

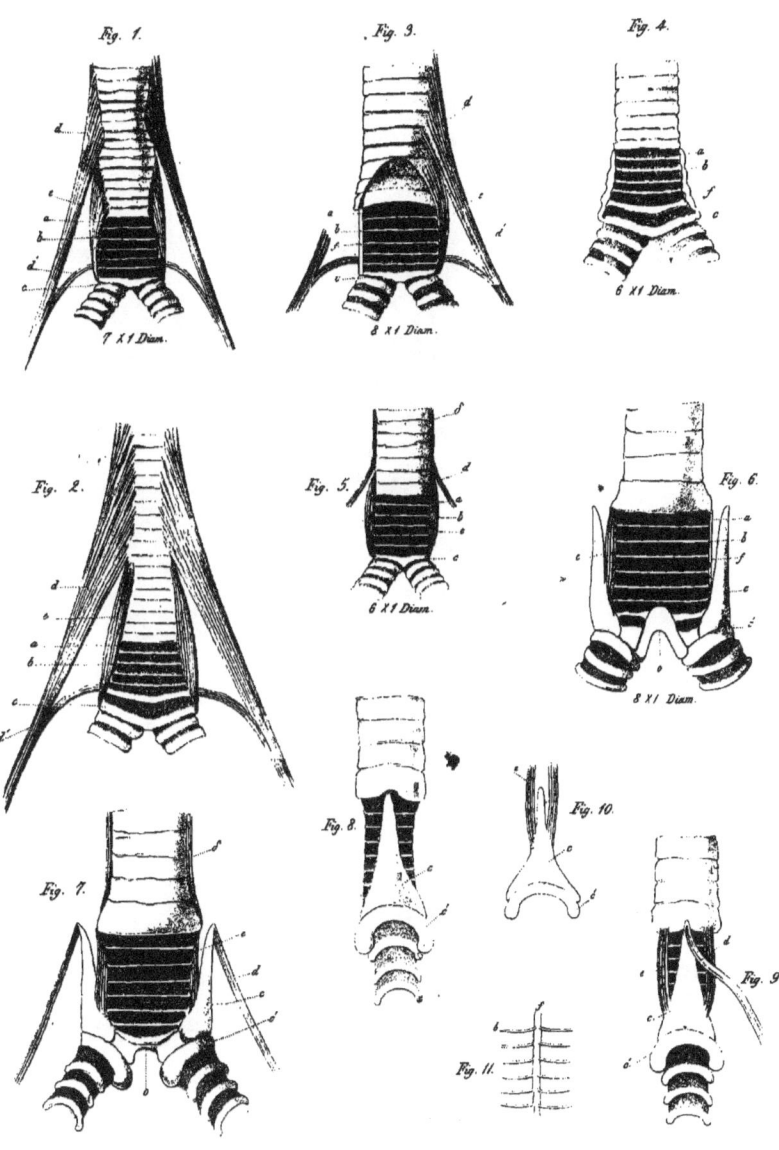

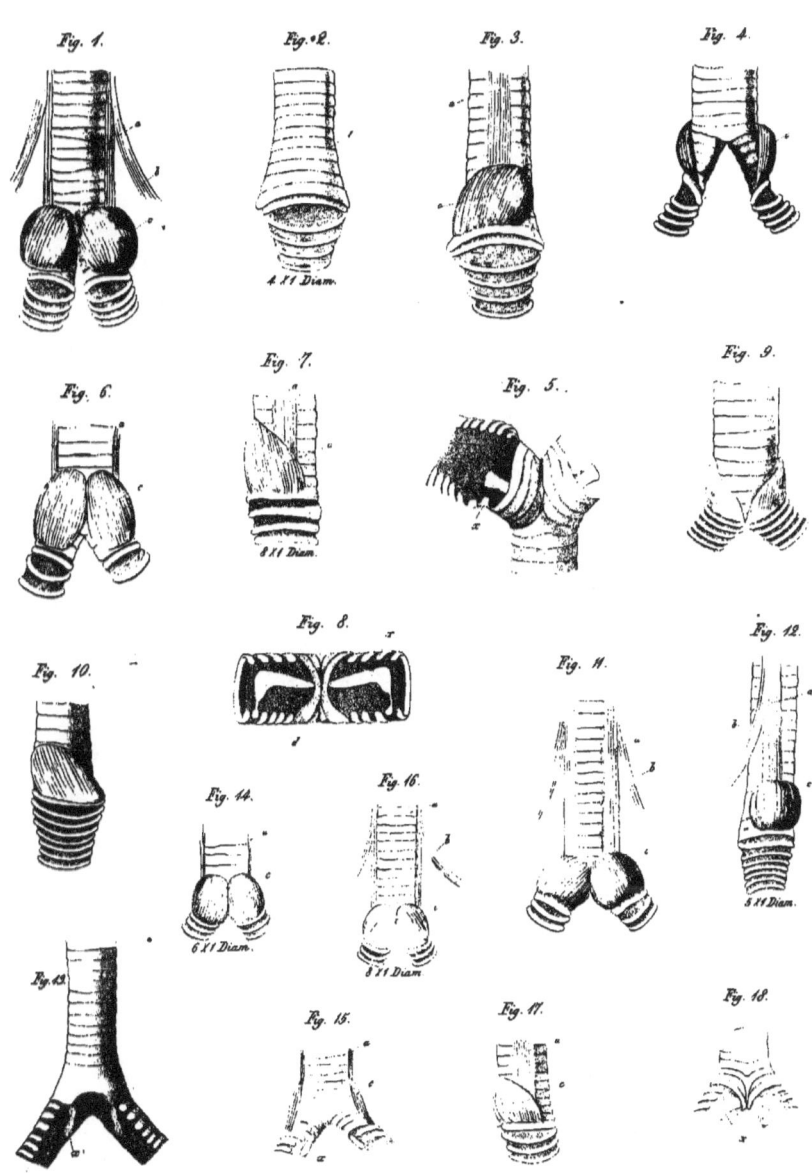

Zu Herrn Müller's Abhandlung über die Stimmorgane. Jahrgang 1835.　　　　Tab. IV.

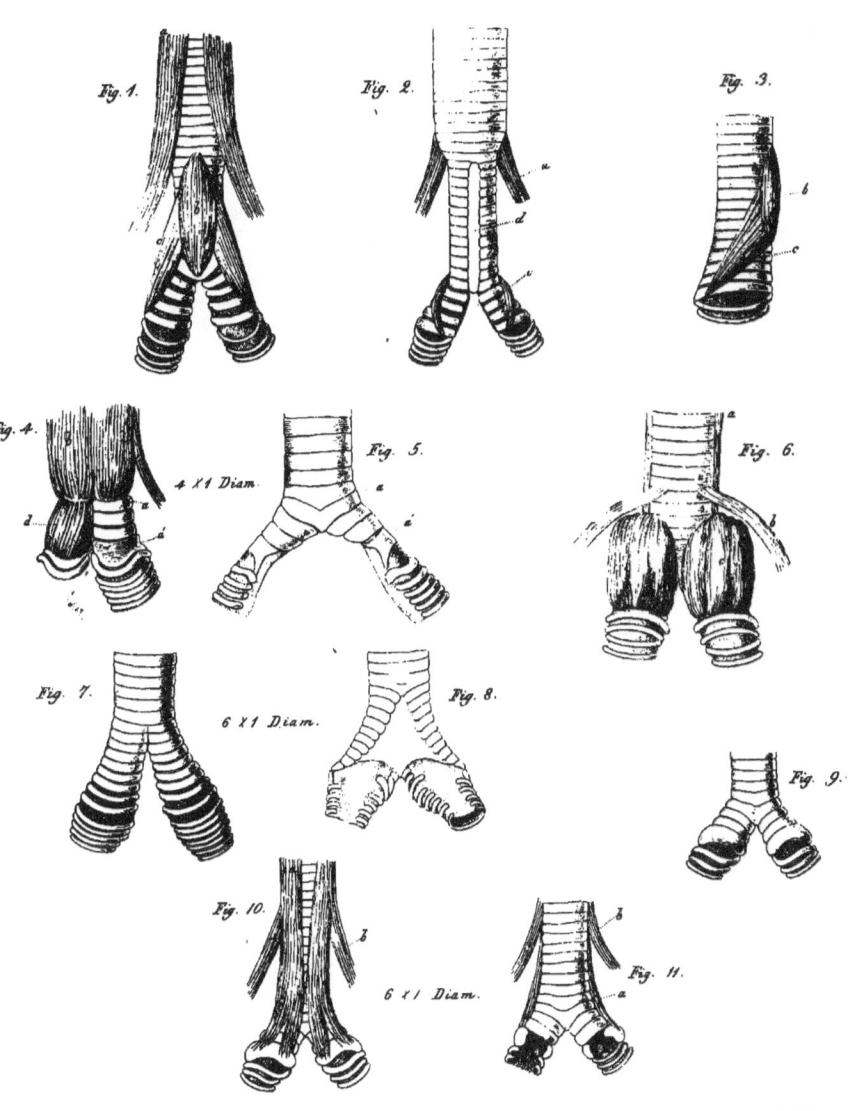

Joh. Müller ad nat. del.　　　　　　　　　　　　　　　　　　　　　　　B. Wenker sc.

Zu Herrn Müller's Abhandlung über die Stimmorgane. Jahrgang 1845. Tab. V.

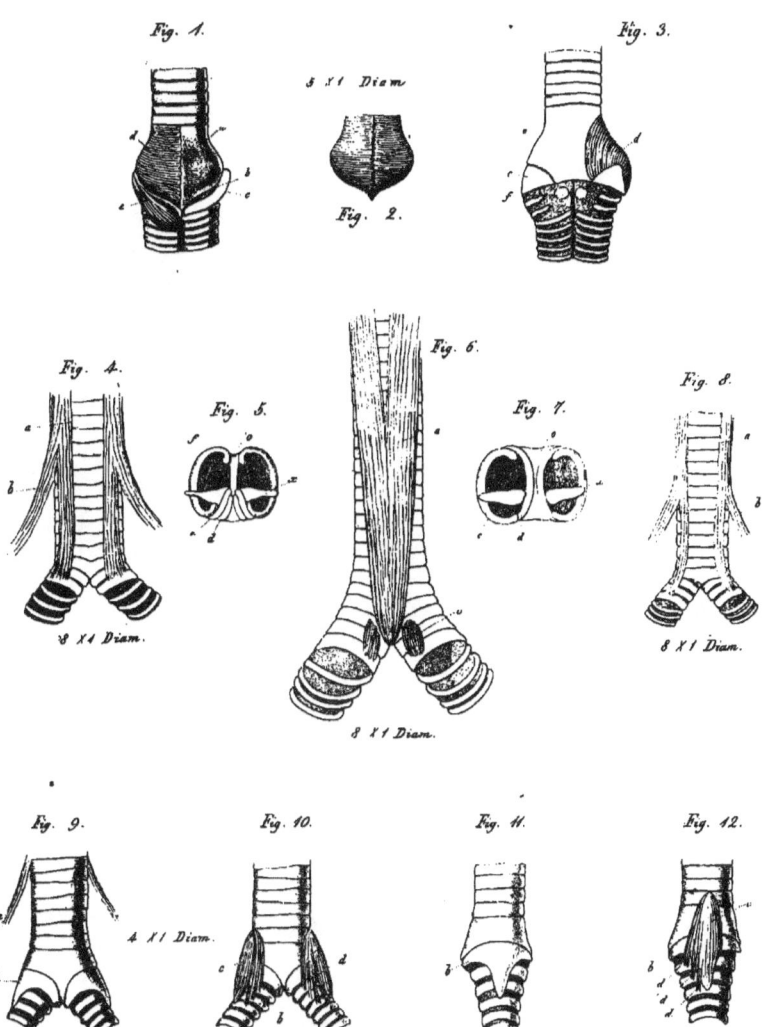

Zu Herrn Müller's Abhandlung über die Stimmorgane. Jahrgang 1845. Tab. VI.

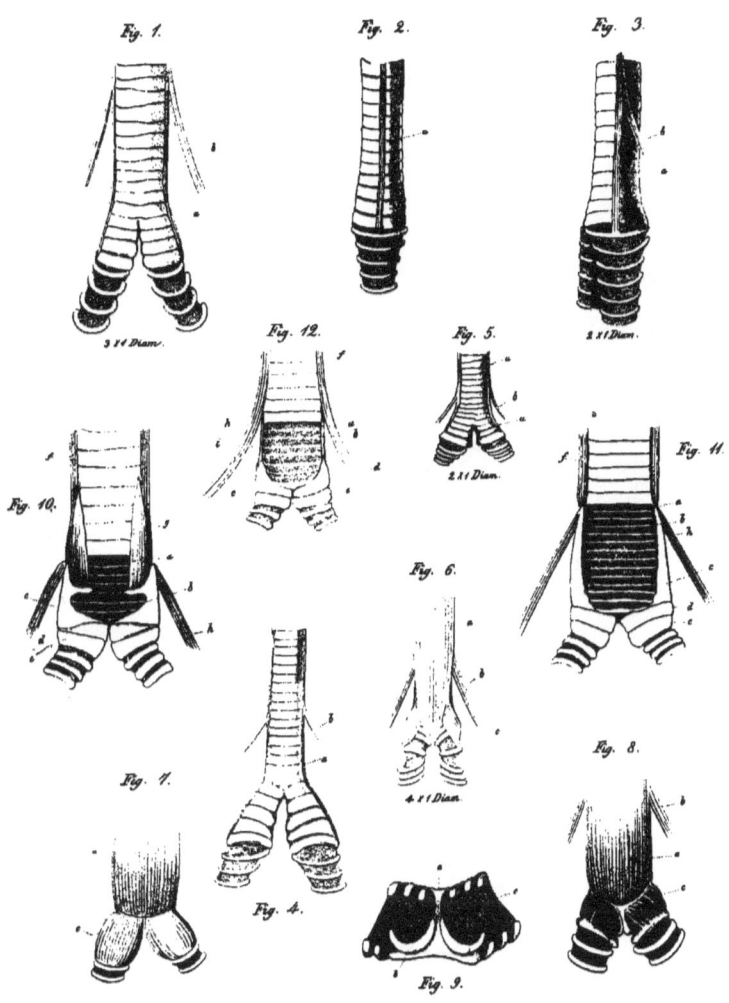

Plate VII.

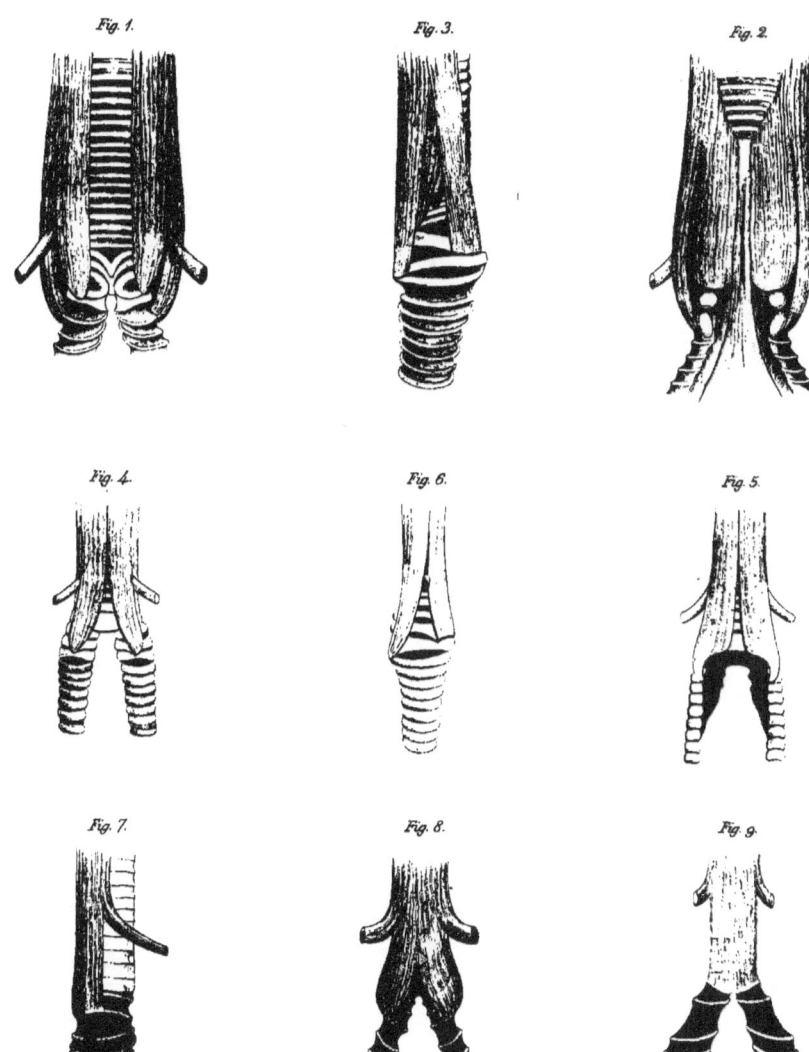

Plate VIII.

London
MACMILLAN AND CO.

PUBLISHERS TO THE UNIVERSITY OF

Oxford

www.ingramcontent.com/pod-product-compliance
Lightning Source LLC
Chambersburg PA
CBHW021947160426
43195CB00011B/1261